T0329195

ation Building in the
Context of
e Zambia One Nation'

Mubanga E. Kashoki

Gadsden Publishers

P O Box 32581, Lusaka, Zambia

ISBN 978 9982 24 1106

CONTENTS

PREFACE

The thoughts, ideas and perspectives brought together under one cover in this work were first expressed on six different occasions as indicated in some detail below. The ideas and perspectives expressed in Chapter 1 were first presented at a seminar on 22 October 2012 organised by Top Floor. Before that, those in Chapter 2 first appeared in 1971, in Volume 2 Number 2 of the *Journal Of The Language Association of Eastern Africa.* This article was later republished with permission in 1990 in *The Factor of Language in Zambia.* Chapters 3 and 4, similarly republished in *The Factor of Language in Zambia,* first appeared in 1973 in *The Bulletin of the Zambia Language Group,* Volume 1 Number 2.

Also included in *The Factor of Language in Zambia* is Chapter 5 which first appeared in *Zango,* a *Zambian Journal of Contemporary Issues* Number 6, in 1976. Chapter 6 first appeared in *Zango* Volume 21 Number 11, in 1977. The latest in the series is Chapter 7 which first appeared in 2007 in the *Journal of Humanities* Volume 7.

The object of bringing all these writings together as a collection of essays on the same subject is to enable the reader to assess the concept of 'One Zambia, One Nation' in a holistic way. More fundamentally, it is to stress the point that the concept has many underlying ramifications and thus requires to be approached with a great deal of philosophical, analytical insight. In other words, it is a concept which is far from being a mere political slogan.

We thank Zambia Education Publishing House for permission to reproduce the chapters in *The Factor of Language in Zambia.*

CHAPTER 1
WHAT IS ZAMBIA'S CULTURAL IDENTITY?*

Introduction
Before attempting a definition of Zambia's cultural identity, it is necessary to begin by giving an account of the historical background that has given shape to Zambia's present identity as a nation state. In this regard, as we know from historical, archeological, ethnographical, linguistic and other sources, the present geographical entity called Zambia came into being as a result of two historical epochs or processes: (i) the precolonial period and (ii) the colonial period.

The Pre-colonial Period
From the evidence available to us, we know that during the pre-colonial period, i.e., the period before Zambia acquired its present territorial boundaries, the present day Zambia, as a piece of land, witnessed a great migration of peoples of Bantu stock from various parts of the central, eastern and southern regions of the African continent who settled within its present day boundaries. It is as the result of this process that we find scattered around the country today such sociocultural groups as the Chewa, Nsenga, Ngoni and Tumbuka in the Eastern province, the Lala and Swaka in the Central province, the Bemba, Bisa, Inamwanga, Lungu and Mambwe in the Northern province, the Aushi, Luunda and Ng'umbo in the Luapula province, the Chokwe, Kaonde, Lunda and Luvale in the North-western province, the Tonga and Ila of Southern Province and the Lozi and Luyana group of peoples in the Western province.

Pre-colonial Migrations
To gain some idea of the migrations of the various indigenous peoples of Zambia prior to colonisation, one needs only to refer to Richard Hall's book, Zambia, published by Pall Mall Press in 1965, which includes headings such as: 'Migrations and Conquest', 'The Lunda Empire', 'The Coming of the Bemba', 'The Lozi enter the valley', 'Mwata Kazembe', 'The Tonga and Ila', and 'The Chewa and Nsenga'.

* These ideas were first presented at a seminar organised by Top Floor on 22/10/12

The Colonial Period

Then came the colonial period. The colonial period is notable for one significant development, namely, that not only did it consolidate the pre-colonial peoples of Zambia into one territorial entity but it predated their birth as a nation state. As we know from history, it was as the result of the Berlin Conference of 1885 and the subsequent partition of Africa into European spheres of influence – the infamous 'Scramble for Africa' – that turned present-day Zambia into its present territorial entity, complete with Caprivi strips and the Congo pedicles. A consequence was the dissecting of sociocultural groups into two parts and assigning one part, unconsulted, to a newly-created nation state across the border. Thus we have at present, for example, Chokwe both in Angola and across the border in Zambia, and similarly, Lamba in Zambia and across the border in the Democratic Republic of the Congo (DRC).

Zambia's Cultural Identity

The overall effect of this is that the sociocultural groups that ended up constituting the geographical entity called Zambia gave rise to a new nation state that was characterised by a great deal of sociocultural diversity, a state of affairs exemplified by the current proliferation of traditional ceremonies. In essence, Zambia in its present state qualifies as a multicultural, multiethnic, multilingual nation state.

Multiculturally, Zambia is a modern nation state endowed with a diversity of cultures rather than with one, monolithic culture. Multi-ethnically, in terms of nationhood, expressed as "One Zambia, One Nation", Zambia is a nation state comprised of diverse peoples or sociocultural groups. Linguistically, too, Zambia is a land of several, though very closely related, languages. Cultural diversity is thus Zambia's defining national character.

It is appropriate by way of summing up to make two points. Firstly, even with respect to the notion of "oneness", diversity is Zambia's defining characteristic as a nation state. Secondly, within the concept of "One Zambia One Nation" as a national motto, diversity ought to be the centrepiece of nationhood, and consequently the point of departure when discussing matters concerning national integration.

CHAPTER 2
LANGUAGE AND NATION IN ZAMBIA VIS-A-VIS NATIONAL INTEGRATION*

The next few pages identify and examine a number of factors which appear in Zambia to have made it difficult for language and the on-going process of national integration to be discussed with any degree of coherence. Part of this difficulty appears to lie in factors which may be related to the recent history of the country. Zambia, like many independent African countries, may be said to have originated in artificial circumstances. The difficulty may, in part, also be attributed to the inadequacies which always attend attempts at definition. One, for example, may ask: What is a 'nation'? Yet another difficulty may find explanation in anthropological legacies whose full impact on the sensibilities of the ordinary citizen are just beginning to be felt. **Tribalism**, whose origin and modern connotations may partly be laid at the door of missionary idealism, colonialism, and nineteenth century anthropology, has considerably contributed to the difficulties which attend attempts at discussing national integration in a rational or detached manner.

The central concern here is with the oft-repeated assertion that national cohesion and national development in the new nations of Africa can only be achieved if ethnic and linguistic loyalties are eliminated or at best minimised. The concern is also with the frequent claim, stated or implied, that amalgamation into an ultimately homogeneous national whole of the various pre-nation (i.e. pre-independence) social and cultural loyalties, including linguistic loyalty, is a pre-condition to the stability of the nation. It is important to state what the central concern is, because to answer whether or not language is an impediment to national unity or national well-being, we need to know in the first place precisely to what kind of unity, stability or integration we are referring.

* First published in 1971 in *The Journal of the Language Association of East Africa*, 2, 2 and reprinted in 1990 in *The Factor of Language in Zambia*.

The Problem

In the mobilisation of the energies and will of the people towards the development of their countries, African governments sooner or later come to grips with the variable popularly known as 'national unity' and otherwise labelled 'national integration'. The mobilisation of the entire indigenous population had been thought to be essential in the struggle against colonialism; it appears no less essential after independence in the ensuing quest for a unified and stable political order. For many multilingual countries, i.e., those in which a multiplicity of diverse languages are used as vehicles of daily communication, the question of language *vis-a-vis* the many varied requirements of a modern state, such as internal cohesion, accelerated development, effective communication systems etc., remains complex and problematic.

The Language Issue in Zambia

In Zambia, if we ignore for the moment the problem of not having an indigenous language acceptable to all as a national language, the overall language problem may be said to fall into four categories:

(i) political (the question of national unity);

(ii) educational (the question of what the medium of instruction should be in the national education system);

(iii) national development and progress (viz., the fear that sentimental attachments to indigenous languages might have a retarding effect on development, more especially in terms of technology, technical expertise, and overall cultural sophistication); and

(iv) national and cultural identity (the concern that loss of one's language, or one's attachment to it, would result in cultural alienation and loss of national uniqueness).

Two main schools of thought may be distinguished:

(a) those who insist on language for development, national progress, national unity, and world communication; and

(b) those who, while acknowledging the importance of language for development and political unity, emphasise language for national and cultural identity, the assertion of the African personality, and continued attachment to the nation's cultural heritage.

4

In a nation such as Zambia, however important the other considerations may be, the quest for integration into the national whole of the various cultural, linguistic and political elements within the national boundaries tends to assume overriding and urgent ascendancy over all others. In this climate of urgency (and anxiety), differences, i.e. the presence of conflict in any form, are often interpreted as an index to the instability of the nation. The absence or removal of conflict is generally assumed to be a necessary pre-condition to the soundness and stability of the national polity. Integration, the process of not just amalgamating, but assimilating into the new nation, previously disparate and autonomous and near autonomous politico-sociocultural entities, has thus become a programme of paramount importance for Zambia.

The need for urgency and haste seems justified, and is certainly understandable, for another very important reason. Politically, Zambia has been described, metaphorically, as an oasis which was surrounded by a desert of hostile governments. To the south, South Africa, during independent Africa's unfinished mission of liberating colonised indigenous populations, represented policies which were directly antithetical to Zambia's and which therefore heightened the chances for mutual suspicion and belligerence. So also was the case before Zimbabwe's political independence in 1980. In Angola and Mozambique, during the era of colonialism, the Portuguese were pursuing a colonial policy to which Zambia was categorically opposed and whose eventual abandonment she openly championed. Here again, the opportunities for mutual antagonism were present in dangerous abundance. The struggle waged in Namibia by the South West African People's Organisation (SWAPO) constituted a military and political challenge on yet another front.

For all these reasons, the task of instilling in the citizenry the sense of oneness and the feeling of solidarity, the feeling of being one people, as a political and psychological measure against external threats, tended in Zambia to assume a ring of absolute and immediate necessity. As a result, the slogan 'United We Stand; Divided We Fall' to a considerable extent lost its contempt, bred of familiarity, and evoked in the national breast an almost religious faith in its relevance.

5

Language, which in the Zambian context is invariably the mark by which the various ethnic communities that constitute the nation can easily be distinguished, found itself at the crossroads of such forces. It was an easy target for those who saw in it the potential for being a divisive factor.

The question the Zambian situation poses is basically the following: Does the existence, or deliberate maintenance, in a nation of a multiplicity of indigenous languages hinder national cohesion? Rephrased, the question becomes in the words of a Television Zambia Programme (ZBS,1971): 'Are Zambian Languages an Impediment to National Unity?'

It is easy to range oneself on one or other side of the question, but such temptation should be resisted, for the simple reason that the question does not permit easy answers. For one thing, there is the ever elusive problem of definition. To be able to come up with pertinent answers (at least answers which do not tend to add to the prevailing confusion), one must to begin with, provide oneself with a satisfactory definition which would at least place such terms as 'nation', 'integration' and 'national unity' in their proper perspective.

Nation: The Problem of Definition

Since the era which gave birth in Europe to the concept of 'nation' and its derivatives 'nationality' and 'nationalism', innumerable attempts at defining these terms have been made, but a general consensus on the adequacy or appropriateness of any one definition does not appear to have been reached, nor is such a general agreement in view. In Zambia, the road to an appropriate definition, and hence a clearer understanding, of the terms has not been made easier by the introduction at independence of 'One Zambia, One Nation' as a national motto. The first and main difficulty is that despite the fact that most of the new nations of Africa originated in very dissimilar historical circumstances from those in which their European counterparts before them did, there is a tendency in Zambia to apply European criteria when describing the 'nationness' of the country.

In Zambia, the general orientation is to regard 'nation' as that condition or stage of nationhood when there is only one language, a common pool of customs, a common set of traditions, or in general a shared national experience. This European-oriented view of 'nation' seems to owe its origin to the:

many writers on political subjects who have used the terms people, nationality and nation', and who have stated that a 'people is a group of individuals who have some objective characteristic in common among which are generally included language, territorial residence, traditions, habits, historical memories and the like, or to the other group of writers who have added to this definition certain subjective elements such as mutual affection, consciousness of difference from other people, or the will to belong to this particular people (Deutsch, 1966: 17).

The result of such an orientation is that the impression is generated that a 'nation', as an authentic and cohesive political community, as differentiated from other similar international communities, must possess a common language, a common history, and a common culture, and, by implication, that until such a stage is attained the nation is not a 'nation; it has still to be built. Hence, it must be supposed, the ubiquitous political shibboleth, 'nation-building', which is quite often interpreted as meaning that the nation does not exist until we have built one or until the preconditions which brought European nations into being are fulfilled.

It is, perhaps, in the light of the above that one may attempt to explain the current search in Zambia for a common cultural identity, the widespread longing for a common medium of communication (a 'national language'), the apparently ill-fated attempt at a common fashion of covering the body, (a 'national dress'), and the incessant call to hotels to include on their menu 'what the people everywhere in the country eat' ('our national dish'). This national groping for common symbols appears to many to represent precisely what is meant by the motto 'One Zambia, One Nation'.

Owing to this predominant reliance on common or shared symbols, many nationals in Zambia are prone to succumb to spasmodic tremors of uncertainty and insecurity when the knowledge of the existence of many languages and sub-cultures within their borders has stared them menacingly in the face. The result is that the most ambivalent policies in the country generally relate to language.

Nation: Towards a definition

Reference has been made to the danger that lies in nations derived essentially from colonialism patterning themselves indiscriminatingly on European models in the search for their own identity. It is commonly acknowledged that colonially derived nations have evolved in ways that are perhaps more artificial or less 'natural' (socioculturally speaking) than were those in which European nations before them originated. In the nations represented by Zambia, the conditions for nationhood which the European-oriented view, the 'common-symbol' model, seems to call for are largely absent. Indeed, such nations are characterised initially (i.e., at independence) by the absence of many of the common factors found in the European model. If common factors exist at all, the list very often will not extend beyond common political boundaries, common political and administrative institutions, a common (often imported) legal system, territorial economic interdependence and interaction, and perhaps the collective effort which may have played a part in the eventual triumph of the indigenous population over the foreign overlord. From one point of view, colonially derived nations may in fact be regarded as a unique phenomenon in the sense that their origins as nation-states have virtually nothing in common with those associated with the former European metropolitan power. It thus seems quite incongruous to insist on a model which at best is of marginal pertinence to one's search for a suitable solution to one's special problems.

The dissimilarity in origin of nationhood touched upon here should lead, at least in the early stages, to the abandonment of the common-symbol model, or at any rate to its appreciation as an essentially irrelevant one on which to pattern one's own 'nation'. A slavish dependence on European models when defining one's own nation may in itself represent an ironical denial of one's claim to nationhood, for if one insists on preconditions which were applicable to Europe, one is in effect denying the *reality* or *existence* of one's own nation.

Chiefly for this reason, the alternative suggested by Fishman *(1968)*, seems to me to offer a more realistic approach to the understanding of 'nation' in the Zambian context. Fishman suggests that the term 'nation' should be reconsidered (merely) 'as a politicogeographic realisation, variously referred to as country, polity or state', adding that in this sense the term need not imply a high degree of sociocultural integration., He also makes the pertinent point that, indeed, nations, as political entities, 'vary greatly in the extent to which they possess such unity within their borders'. (Fishman, Ferguson and Das Gupta, *1968:* 39).

An important point for the purpose of the present argument must be underlined here. Fishman's approach to definition emphasises the reality of 'nation' and, as he himself points out a few lines further on in the same article, avoids confusing questions of political community and socio-cultural community which, though related, are quite independent, (ibid : 39).

This approach is also useful in at least two other respects. On the one hand, it enables one to discard the European model, and, on the other hand, it makes it possible for one to see that sociocultural integration (as distinct from national consciousness, that is, how a people perceive themselves as a nation and how they feel about belonging to that nation) in colonially derived nations is a process whose fulfilment may take place *within* the reality of the political community or 'nation', and which will almost invariably be achieved *after* independence. Fishman has called this process 'nationality'. Because this is a crucial aspect in the present argument, I quote Fishman here in full:

Nationality might best be reconsidered as a sociocultural entity that may have no corresponding politicogeographic realisation. Its discriminanda are essentially at the level of authenticity and solidarity of group behaviors and group values, rather than at the level of governmental, politico-geographic realisations and implementations. The advantage of separating these two kinds of national integration (both terminologically and conceptually) is that such separation provides greater insight into why social solidarity is not a precondition for the existence of a national political community and into how a national political community can attain solidarity in successive steps (Fishman, Ferguson and Das Gupta, 1969: 39).

9

Integration: The problem of definition

Thus, when it comes to the term 'integration' the fundamental question to pose is: What exactly is meant by 'nation-building' in the context of a colonially derived nation? In other words what precisely does one mean by 'One Zambia' in the first part of the Zambian national motto? What are the implications in terms of integration?

From what we have seen, it seems to me that what is involved is essentially the transformation of traditional ethnic loyalties, real or imagined, into new and perhaps ultimately homogenous, national loyalties. This process presupposes the acquisition of common values, aspirations and sentiments by the members of the nation so that after a period, which may be short or protracted, the nation comes not only to strengthen what has frequently been termed 'a national consciousness' but also to acquire a reasonable degree of sociocultural integration. Sociocultural integration, however, should be distinguished from its sister term 'national unity' which almost always has political overtones. It is important to make this distinction. The presence of a national consciousness and sociocultural integration in a nation may not necessarily result in *political* unity and yet one often gets the impression that almost without exception national leaders and party functionaries in developing nations view integration primarily in political terms. It is perhaps due to this preoccupation with political viewpoints that many of these leaders tend to assume that a one-party system, seen essentially as a tool in that direction, is an important condition for the unification of their peoples.

In this section of the argument, in discussing language and national integration, it is the sociocultural and not the political solidarity that will receive emphasis. I take it that as long as political differences remain of a nature that does not seriously endanger the very fabric or existence of the nation, then such differences may even be desirable.

The road to national integration and the means of arriving there is complicated, in Zambia, by several related variables. For economy of time and space only one or two will be touched upon here.

In Zambia's active quest for a stronger national consciousness, where allegiance to the central government and loyalty to the nation are deemed to be subordinate to none, and where regional or fragmented loyalties are a cause of suspicion and apprehension, the tendency, it seems to me, has been for many compatriots with whom I have discussed the problem to imagine that all loyalties, linguistic, cultural, political etc., which antedated newly-induced (i.e., post-independence) loyalties, are static, immutable, or incapable of being alloyed. For that reason, they are seen as posing a real threat to the future of the national government and national sentiments.

In the grip of this apprehension, the point seems to be completely lost that loyalty or allegiance cannot be conceived of as a static or immutable condition. The point also seems to me to have received little appreciation that several levels and even kinds of loyalty can coexist in one person, and that the only question is which group loyalty takes priority in a given social situation. (Cf. Molteno, 1974, for a more extended exposition of the point). I think that what has still to be appreciated more generally than it is now is that, even in the past rarely did cultural, social, or political allegiances crystallize to a point where they became absolutely rigid and immutable. These allegiances often underwent and resulted in new orientations. The Bemba-speaking people for example, could owe allegiance to their local chief (e.g. Chief Makasa) and simultaneously to the "over-all" chief, the *primus inter pares,* Chitimukulu, who at a higher level symbolised the unifying factor culturally, politically, as well as in terms of religion (cf. Meebelo, 1971, especially Chapter II. pp. 25-71.)

In the same way, it is possible for a person today to owe allegiance to the traditional ruler (i.e., the chief) and simultaneously to the new political leader and administrator. In short, loyalty should be perceived as a relative and circumstantial condition: it is, as has been stated above, expressed in accordance with the dictates of the particular social situation. In one situation the individual may find that the social circumstances require him to show allegiance to the local chief; in another he may have to shift his loyalty to a higher authority. Such allegiances, however, are not necessarily inimical to each other; they may crisscross but they are not necessarily at cross purposes. Moreover, loyalty to the chief, or to one's small group, and that to the national leader or to the national group, are never absolute nor mutually exclusive. In any case, no state (not even that under the iron hand of a dictator) can always boast the absolute or undivided loyalty of all its citizens. It is, however, because allegiance and loyalty are not widely seen in this light that an increasingly one-language-oriented group, though not yet very vocal, is emerging in Zambia.

Another difficulty in the perception of oneness which may be mentioned here is what I can only describe as utopian visions or notions on the part of some Zambians, notions which seem to regard 'oneness' as some sort of perfect state in which all differences are eventually eliminated, and in which everybody lives in absolute harmony and complete unity. Apparently on the strength of such notions, I quite frequently get the question: 'I understand you are carrying out research into Zambian languages. When are you people at the university going to give us one language so that we can become one nation?' Or the question is somewhat obliquely asked 'Are you working on a language like Esperanto which might give us one language eventually?'

There is implicit in this question the assumption that integration takes place chiefly through, as stated earlier, the availability and use of one common language, and the minimisation of the role of other factors, educational, social, religious etc., which daily influence the direction and pace of integration. The assumption sometimes leads to the interesting argument that were one language to be set aside as a national language in a firm, unequivocal decision, then integration would proceed more quickly and in the desirable direction. The possibility, if it is ever pondered, that such a decision might in fact introduce divisive tendencies, or in no way alter the course or pace of integration, seems to receive scant consideration.

The final difficulty that may be considered here is that relating to the discussion of integration almost always from the point of view of the urban area – the melting pot. Most discussions of integration in Zambia do not appear to take the rural variable sufficiently into account, for in any question of integration it is necessary to make a distinction between the urban and the rural areas.

In rural areas in Zambia, the pressure, or even the need, to integrate is never very great as most communities when considered in their local setting, are socioculturally inward and not outward looking. They already enjoy the advantage of deep-rooted sociocultural ties, a common language, a common culture, and more or less a common traditional political system. True, each of the ten administrative provincial divisions of Zambia is populated by different sociocultural groups speaking a variety of dialects, some mutually intelligible, others virtually mutually incomprehensible. But it is also the case that, generally speaking, these communities and their languages are restricted to certain specific areas and are only in some instances in the hodgepodge mixture that one very often encounters in the urban environment. In the rural areas, contact with other linguistic groups except in border situations and in areas represented by Kabompo and Zambezi districts is minimal, if not non-existent. In such a situation, the need does not arise requiring the individual to make certain sociocultural concessions in order to accommodate individuals of a different sociocultural background, at least not to the same extent that it does in urban areas. It is obvious that in these areas integration into the national fabric will proceed slowly and will take a long time to achieve.

In urban areas, on the contrary, people are constantly coming into contact with persons of a dissimilar sociocultural background, and in consequence are having to learn a variety of languages in order to cope with a highly multilingual situation. At the same time, different cultures are interacting and social co-mingling is significant with an increasing number of the young generation marrying across tribal or linguistic boundaries. It is here that the problem of integration is most acute.

Integration: The problem of language
In the period immediately following independence, Zambia like most of the new nations of Africa, has found herself faced with two major tasks which remained submerged while attention was focused on the elimination of colonialism, but which soon emerged with pressing urgency once the fight had been won. The tasks may simply be stated as national unification (involving the unification politically of pre-nation diverse cultural or linguistic elements) and national development (involving the modernisation of the politico-sociocultural and economic institutions of the nation).

In carrying out each of these tasks, language is seen as an important factor. In the Zambian context particularly, language is a crucial factor because of the multiplicity of languages in use in the country. The prevailing linguistic situation is not yet very clear, but it is safe to state that there are about twenty indigenous languages which are not mutually intelligible. This fact alone makes internal communication difficult and even when only a number out of the several languages is selected for limited communication and educational purposes, the problem is not minimised: indeed, in some respects it is made more complicated as when it introduces conflicts as to which ones should be included and which ones should be left out.

If internal communication were the only factor to consider, multilingualism in Zambia would not be such a vexing problem. Unfortunately, language is frequently seen not merely as a vehicle of communication but as the prime if not the only characteristic by which the various ethnic communities making up the nation can easily be identified. Language, in other words, is seen as one of the more important ties which bind people to their pre-nation sociocultural units. It is also seen as a factor which, if left unmodified, can perpetuate and intensify sectional cleavages. Consequently the pervasive belief reasserts itself that if national integration (i.e. a common sociocultural orientation) is to come about a common language must first be adopted. This belief is reinforced by another widely held belief that linguistic divisions are really at the root of political divisions. The fact that the belief is not consonant or is only partly so with reality is not germane to the issue.

It should also be remembered that prior to independence, a foreign language – English – had functioned as an effective link between leaders of the independence struggle belonging to different cultural or linguistic backgrounds. When eventually these leaders emerged as national leaders, it was natural for them to regard the language which had seemed to unite them as an indispensable unifying factor. When one also bears in mind that English has been employed before and after independence for national and international communication, it is understandable that a prominent politician and a former Minister of Education should write:

> *All leaders now accept that the real strength of national unity*
> *lies in the recognition of the legitimate hopes and fears as*
> *well as the interests of the diverse elements, which constitute*
> *the Zambian nation - that is the several tribes scattered in all*

parts of the country. It is unity in diversity which is being forged without exacerbating inter-tribal conflicts and suspicions which have disruptive effect. Because of this fact, even the most ardent nationalists of our time have accepted the inevitable fact that English – ironically a foreign language and also the language of our former colonial masters – has definitely a unifying role in Zambia (Mwanakatwe, (1968: 213).

It is instructive to note that, however one interprets the above observation, it is political and not sociocultural unity that is uppermost in the mind of the writer. It is significant also that English is hailed, however reluctantly, as a unifying factor mainly because it has been used both before and after independence for business transactions, internally as well as externally and for legislation and education. Here Mwanakatwe observes:

It is the language used by the administration at all levels ... in parliament, in the Courts, at meetings of municipal and township councils, in the more advanced industrial and commercial institutions, the banks, post offices and others - English is an effective instrument for the transaction of business (ibid: 213).

English has thus occupied a unique position in the life of the Zambian people especially that of the Zambian elite, who in any case is the person who matters when questions of language are debated. English has also occupied a central position as far as the political unification and national development of the country are concerned. It is therefore easy to conclude that it is the instrument and perhaps the only one, for 'national unity'.

On the other hand, since indigenous languages on the whole have not occupied such a favourable position, but have been relegated to marginal areas of internal communication, and have at the same time been confined to the more rudimentary types of primary and adult education, and their use in the conduct of government has been restricted to local courts and traditional forms of administration, it is only to be expected that they should project a negative image. It is certainly not surprising that a former Minister of State for Technical Education and Vocational Training should declare:

In order to achieve our objective of national strength and progress the youth must at the very outset be armed with knowledge that will equip them with the initiative and knowledge to compete with the world at large. In the pursuit of this objective therefore the trappings of syllabuses searching for national identity must take second place and those in search of universal identity and the applicable knowledge ensuring national technical capability must take the first place. (Musakanya, 1970: 37).

Moreover, since indigenous languages have not been encouraged to a level where one of them could successfully dislodge English either for internal national communication or for educational purposes, they are not regarded as valuable assets for national integration. Their usefulness is not only peripheral to much of what the nation does, but such usefulness as there may be is frequently of a localised nature.

These facts considered together cause indigenous languages to seem unsuitable as instruments of national unification, culturally but more especially politically.

Integration: The role of language
It should be apparent from the foregoing that the role language can play in sociocultural integration depends very largely on the form we envisage such integration to take: the assimilative (or 'homogenising') type or the pluralistic (or *laissez faire*) type. One policy may consciously aim at eliminating all cultural differences as the most desirable path to national integration. Obviously, encouraging the active use of a diversity of languages would be incompatible with such a policy. On the other hand, a different policy may take into account the highly complex sociocultural diversity of most of the newly independent African states and may for this reason decide on a policy that aims at accommodating such diversity. Needless to say, such a policy would sooner or later have to come to grips with the problem not only of **multiculturalism** but of **multilingualism** as well. The latter rather than aiming at elimination would merely attempt to minimise the existing sociocultural differences. Each of these choices is strewn with thorny issues and the ultimate goal can only be reached after a great deal of careful thinking and policy adjustment throughout the period of implementation.

In the Zambian context, if one is to take Mwanakatwe's statement (already cited) as representative of government thinking, it is 'unity in diversity' that the government seems to aim at fostering. Such a view, if indeed it is representative, appears to recognize that complete 'homogenisation' or assimilation of a conglomerate of diverse sociocultural groups is not possible and that the only alternative may well be to accept the existing diversity, to accommodate such diversity, and to tailor all planning to the policy of accommodation.

Be this as it may, the present government language policy includes for use in education and internal communication seven of the more widely spoken and understood languages, Icibemba, Kikaonde, Silozi, Luvale, Lunda, Cinyanja and Chitonga. Of these, Chitonga and Silozi, but more especially Cibemba and Cinyanja, are becoming instruments of wider communication outside of their traditional environs and are increasingly playing an important role in the sociocultural integration of the people. The relevance and significance of this assertion is underlined by the evidence presented in Chapters 5 and 6.

In town, loss of one's once strong tribal anchorage is being achieved mainly through ties of intermarriage, through neighbour-to-neighbour interaction, or through growing up either at school or at home among peers from different tribal backgrounds. Each of these processes is to a lesser or greater extent without the aid of English as an integrating factor. Even those who insist on the overwhelming usefulness and importance of English are coming to admit that such usefulness and importance, at least for the time being, is only true for a very small, though influential, minority of the population.

Although the point raised here is not easy to demonstrate in quantitative terms, much less so objectively, one could risk the assertion that the human interaction just described as taking place in the urban areas of Zambia – the so-called melting pot – is more meaningful in high-density than in low-density townships. In Lusaka, to give a more familiar example, the medium of communication in high-density townships is, generally speaking, indigenous languages, while in low-density areas most communication among the residents is conducted in English. In both high-density and low-density townships, several tribes, speaking a variety of languages and observing differing customs, have been brought together. In both sociocultural integration is taking place.

In low-density townships, however, it is generally acknowledged that perhaps because of the elitist attitudes prevailing there and a preponderance towards a foreign mode of life, whatever sociocultural integration is taking place remains superficial, impersonal, and lacking in certain characteristics which give high-density townships their special character: the perpetuation of the more intimate and more personal human relationships that village life so characteristically embodies. Moreover residents in low-density townships in general tend to be more aware of the ethnic differences that exist between them even though they are in the main using a common means of communication, namely English.

In high-density townships, on the other hand the keen ethnic sensitivity which is observable in low-density areas is not so pronounced. But this is not in any way intended to suggest that members of the lower income groups (who are also generally less educated than those in higher income groups) are not conscious of their ethnic origins. They are, but theirs, it would appear, is a less deeply cultivated and more diffusely articulated consciousness than that which one may observe among the more educationally privileged and, as it happens the more economically advantaged. From this point of view, the problem may in general point to an ironical twist of circumstance, namely that as one becomes more educated, the more keenly different one feels from those of other ethnic backgrounds.

Thus, while English may serve as a very effective tool for internal and international communication, and while it may be a significant factor in the development process, its role as an integrating tool, socially and culturally, remains rather superficial and marginal even for the minority that uses it.

The point is worth appreciating also that access to and the use of one language by all the members of the nation, although admittedly a useful ingredient in the integration process, does not in itself lead to the removal of ethnic labels and attitudes. This is clearly illustrated by the case of the United States where despite the use of one common language, the population continues to be divided into hyphenated groupings – a persistent reminder of the ethnic composition of the American nation. It is quite likely then, that in multi-ethnic nations such as Zambia, it is not mere speculation that even were the people eventually to speak one language, the labels applicable today, Bemba, Kaonde, Lozi, etc. might exhibit a tenacity as that now evident in the United States. In any case labels in themselves are innocuous: it is only when they are exploited for whatever reason that they become of detriment to society and therefore objectionable, a point to which we return in Chapter 5.

The case for maintaining, and even encouraging, linguistic diversity while employing one language for certain aspects of the country's administration is strengthened by the Swiss experience. Although in Belgium the experience has not been an entirely happy one, in Switzerland a sense of oneness has been achieved despite the fact that four different languages (French, German, Rhaeto-Romansch and Italian) have been maintained officially as vehicles of national communication.

There is, however, the argument by Fishman that indigenous languages may be an important integrative force but only in the short term. 'It is out of the long-term process of living with and transmuting a modern foreign technology and a modern foreign language (and the foreign life style to which both are anchored)', he contends, 'that the future sociocultural integration of the 'new' nation' will come'. With the introduction in Zambia, in 1965, of English as the medium of instruction throughout primary, secondary, and higher education, coupled with the special status of the language in most of the more important functions of the nation, Fishman's prediction might indeed be indicative of things to come.

Even so, it is doubtful given the tenacious nature of language, that indigenous languages in Zambia will be replaced entirely by English in the foreseeable future. After all, as indicated earlier, several of them are progressively becoming *linguae francae* within the national boundaries. As I see it, what is likely to happen is that, especially considering the resources and efforts being allocated to the promotion of English as a national and international means of communication, a foreign language will continue to dominate the scene while indigenous languages will continue for some time (how long, it is difficult to say) in their role as vehicles for regional or provincial communication. In view of this, the cause of integration, in my opinion, may be better served if the limitations of both English and indigenous languages are recognised and appropriate measures are taken to encourage nationals to master two or more indigenous languages in addition to their mastery of the language of wider communication. This measure, it seems to me, would have the advantage of enabling the national to communicate with a wider spectrum of compatriots than is the case at the moment. Ability to speak English (and presumably one's own mother tongue) severely limits one to a small section of the population; ability to speak several indigenous languages enhances one's chances of reaching a wider audience, thereby multiplying the opportunities for greater sociocultural integration within one's society.

NOTES

1 High-density and low-density are terms used to describe areas in which low and high income groups respectively reside in the major towns of Zambia.

2 For predictions of how the language problems might be solved in the new nations see Joshua A Fishman 'Language Problems and Types of Political and Sociocultural Integration' in *Language Problems of Developing Nations,* Fishman, Ferguson and Das Gupta 1969.

CHAPTER 3
THE DILEMMA OF NATIONAL INTEGRATION*

In many independent African countries today, where a multilingual and multicultural situation exists, there is a constant and as often as not a frantic search for sociocultural integration. In this search, certain salient factors have tended to receive scant attention and it is the purpose of this chapter to discuss at some length some of these factors.

As quoted by Fishman (1971), Gadgil (1955) has observed that the real problem of underdeveloped countries is that of finding the terms on which they can coexist honourably with the technology and civilisation of the West. There is no question of rejecting the latter: at the same time, however, it is not possible for these societies to accept the West completely, to forget their own past (p. 45). Stated in this fashion, the selection of the relevant road to an honourable future becomes both a dilemma and a challenge. As a dilemma, it might lead, as it has already done in so many cases, to considerable ambivalence or lack of a clear sense of direction among policymakers with regard to the goals and strategies to be adopted. As a challenge it might require of the policymakers a high degree of dexterity of mind (to enable them to consider all the options available), clarity of vision (to enable them to arrive at the optimum choice and to discard the irrelevant) and boldness of decision (a necessary condition for sticking only to what one believes to be right and in the public good).

If the problem inherent in charting goals and strategies calculated to ensure a stable but progressive society - politically, socially, culturally and economically - appears almost intractable, the problem is no less intractable when it is merely that of language. In countries such as Zambia and others similarly placed, where society is faced with a multiplicity of languages, which directly or indirectly affect its various resources and the manner in and the extent to which they are utilised, one imperative seems inescapable: the need to arrive at a clear policy to guide the nation in its proper use of the various languages at its disposal.

* First published in 1990 in *The Factor of Language in Zambia.*

21

In many countries in Africa, all too often the call for a clear language policy is easier in the proposition than in the execution. In these countries their respective linguistic situations are so complex and so varied that each situation is best considered and decided on its own merit, while of course not completely discarding the comparative approach to the problem. In Zambia, the dilemma and the challenge alluded to earlier seem to derive from problems which may be enumerated as follows.

Most importantly, 'what in fact is meant by *national integration,* or as Zambia's national motto states by 'One Zambia, One Nation' not only as a concept but as a process? When one says, 'One Zambia, One Nation' what precisely does one mean by the two phrases? In order to achieve Zambia's goal of 'One Zambia, One Nation,' how does one intend to go about it? And what product is envisaged at the end of the process? These seemingly repetitive rhetorical questions are basic and pertinent to the consideration of the role one envisages language to play in shaping the Zambian society into a wholesome whole.

One needs to know whether the aim is consciously to evolve a nation in which eventually there will be no traces whatsoever of erstwhile tribal affiliations, or whether the aim is merely to create a nation whose main characteristics are accommodation, tolerance, and mutual respect among the various ethnic communities, i.e. integration characterised by diversity. The absence of a precise rationale as regards the sociocultural integration one envisages for the Zambian society and the means of achieving it is paralleled by a tendency, quite widespread in the country, especially in political circles, of confusing *political integration* (or the political evolution of and ensuring a stable order) with *sociocultural integration,* two related but quite distinct processes. As used and elaborated by Fishman (1971: 28-45), the former has to do with 'operational efficiency' (i.e., 'effectiveness in the realms of public order and public service, as well as industrially, commercially, educationally, diplomatically, and militarily'); and the latter with ethnic authenticity or cultural identity (or what I consider to be the consolidation of a national consciousness). Thus, one is predominantly administrative and technological, while the other is predominantly sociocultural in nature. The problem here is the frequent assumption that political unity means cultural integration and that both can be achieved by adopting, essentially, the same strategies and tactics.

In adopting strategies for achieving effective sociocultural integration, there is what appears to be an underlying philosophy in Zambia, namely that integration means, as we saw in Chapter 2, the search for common symbols, and that once these have been secured, national integration is as good as secured as well. It seems to me that such an assumption misses an important point, which is that Zambia is a multitribal, multicultural and multilingual society, and that this condition is likely to persist for generations to come. Given this likelihood, it is surprising that, in seeking relevant solutions to our problems, those of us in Africa seem to set our minds on what I consider to be the most elusive solution of all; *uniformity* or sameness, rather than *diversity*. While our situations, culturally and linguistically, are characterised by a high degree of diversity, we still want a national culture, a national pool of customs, a national *dish,* a national *dress* (for women), a national *bush suit* (for men), and above all a transcendent *supra-tribe* (i.e. a 'tribeless' nation) and a *national language* in the same way that we talk of a national president, a national assembly, a national emblem and a national motto. We appear to regard as inconceivable the evolution of national *cultures,* national *dishes,* national *bush suits,* national *tribes,* and national *languages* (if only in the sense that they are all properties of the nation). Our present orientation appears to dictate that diversity must always give way to uniformity, for apparently in uniformity there is national unity, and in diversity national disunity.

Here, as I see it, the problem is that we find what appear to us to be soft options – the line of least resistance – more appealing than hard options. In any case, there is a tendency to run away from the reality of our situation, its complexity and the special considerations and handling that it requires. What seems to be most attractive to us is for example, the equation that One (National) Language = 'One Zambia, One Nation', The difficulty here is, of course, that such an equation obscures the fundamental point that while $4 - 3 = 1$, English minus all Zambian languages may not necessarily result in national integration or even political unity.

The tendency towards uniformity, sameness, or oneness in Zambia is understandable. It stems from a mortal fear of that dreadful pestilence, referred to in sociological, anthropological, and political journals as *tribalism*. As is well known today, tribalism (believed to be an epidemic of continental proportions) has become a veritable paranoia of Africa. In most African countries, tribalism is a subject one would rather not talk about, except on those frequent occasions when one wishes to impute its practice to others but never to oneself. In any case, in multilingual countries the mere mention of tribalism prejudices even the most innocent of discussions about language.

In the context of our argument, the problem is that language is very often assumed to be synonymous with *tribe,* so that, for example, the Lozi language is associated only with the Lozi tribe, the Bemba language with the Bemba tribe, and so on. The transition from *tribe* to *tribalism* is but a simple operation, for isn't tribalism (in the minds of many) the immediate consequence of tribe? The effect of this is that we arrive at another popular sociopolitical equation: Language = Tribe = Tribalism. The fact that very few languages, if any, are spoken only by members associated 'tribally' with those languages is glossed over in the national interest.

The point being made is this: almost invariably any allusion to indigenous languages and their role in social, cultural and political integration instantly conjures up images, or rather nightmares, of rampant tribalism, especially if deliberate political capital is made of the popular (but mistaken) notion that 'there are 73 languages in Zambia'. Very often, the emphasis on '73' is intended to reinforce or exploit the idea that one cannot encourage such 'extreme' diversity without running the danger of exacerbating tribal differences. Thus, by implication, the appeal is instead to the 'minimisation' of tribal differences, including linguistic differences. Hence, all roads should be diverted deliberately to One Language – a national language – for in 'oneness', as we have seen, there is believed to be unity.

Alongside the paranoid dread of tribalism is the tendency to confuse communication (national as well as international, i.e., operational efficiency) with integration. It is often assumed, for example, that because English can be used as an efficient means of communication between different communities speaking different languages, and also for administering the country, it is *ipso facto* an efficient instrument for uniting or integrating those communities. Whether the one necessarily results into the other is, of course, debatable. One can think of a number of countries where though one language is in operation, political, and even sociocultural integration remain elusive.

Granted, if a government is to administer a country efficiently, it requires an efficient means of communication to achieve this, and obviously, the use of a common language makes this possible. The use of many languages for the same purpose is not only cumbersome and possibly inefficient, but time-consuming and costly. But easier and more efficient communication is by no means the same as, or at any rate a substitute for, integration, even though facilitated national communication may lead to national integration. The latter is only the consequence of the former and is no substitute.

Again, here, we must harp back to our previous proposition, namely the constant groping for national symbols. The preoccupation with national symbols makes it tempting to assume that the use of one language – in our case English – is the only sensible road to national integration. In this context, Zambian languages are quite often thought of as evil forces insofar as national integration is concerned. With their immediate association with tribalism, they are easily imbued in the public eye with divisive tendencies. For example, the conclusion reached during a television programme, (Topic, 26 May, 1971), in which the discussion was whether Zambian languages hindered or promoted national unity, was that they most definitely worked *against* national unity.

Then there is the haste with which multi-ethnic countries seem to be pressing forward with national integration. Particularly in Zambia, an additional problem in our current programme of national integration is our tendency to labour under the impression that integration can be achieved in 'a matter of weeks rather than months', to quote a Wilsonian prophecy that never came true.

This haste has historical precedents in the Zambian society, and from that standpoint is understandable. Independence from foreign domination had been won in the space of a little more than fifty years. Then, after independence, one could with justifiable pride point to the proliferation of schools, factories, roads, etc., in less than ten years as a clear indication that accelerated progress is possible and can be initiated and stimulated by conscious planning. It is perhaps not surprising that one frequently encounters the sentiment that in the same way one could resolve one's cultural and social problems in a matter of weeks rather than decades. This apparent haste seems to miss a vital point, namely that national integration is a complex process involving, as it does, many and diverse (and even conflicting) factors for its attainment. In its handling it requires not only flexibility but, above all, patience. In any case, there are enough lessons from the African past to remind us that cultural and linguistic diversities have been realities in Africa for a very long time, and it is unlikely that this situation will change appreciably in the foreseeable future. It is clear then that, however fervently we may wish the multilingual problem away, we will be stuck with it for generations to come.

Additional to the difficulties so far enumerated, there is the related problem that, because English has been proclaimed as the official language to be used for the more important functions of the state, it is generally assumed that it is at the same time the language the citizens employ in their inter-personal relations: in the home, at play, at family gatherings, away from school, away from work, etc. In the absence of definitive conclusive evidence it would appear that, rather than English, it is the Zambian languages which are playing a more significant role in these contexts, and one would assume, therefore, that they are the more important integrative instruments in this regard.

Comparing the Zambian situation with situations elsewhere, the formerly rigid class system (e.g. the barrier between the middle class and the aristocracy) in Britain might be a good example, for our present purposes, of situations where social and even cultural barriers are not necessarily removed by the possession and use of a common medium of communication. Relating this to our own situation, we may find that English, while serving as an efficient means of communication, may do very little to minimise what some choose to refer to as 'tribal' cleavages that might be evident in the country. In that case, we would need to consider additional or alternative means of integrating the society. Are Zambian languages one such alternative?

At this point, there are two final problems to consider. The first relates to the confidence, in nations where English is used as the official language, in the English language (invariably acquired through the school system) as an indispensable integrative force. This confidence would not be so inordinately misplaced if, in these nations, one had a school system that would enable one to implement a programme of universal education. As it is, human, financial, and material resources make it virtually impossible for these nations to implement such a programme. Moreover, there is the problem of the evergrowing population, which adds to the strain on the already limited capacity to maintain viable social services. All this means that in countries which are the focus of our attention, we shall be unable to provide education – in effect a knowledge of English – to all our people for a number of generations to come. This being the case, it is pertinent to pose the question: how do we hope to integrate into the national fabric that segment of our society that will have no access whatsoever to the English language – our current panacea for all problems of national integration?

Related to the foregoing, and perhaps in some ways the direct consequence of it, is the problem of the educated-uneducated gap (not to speak of the now legendary urban-rural and generation gaps). What means do we intend to employ to build appropriate bridges of social and cultural integration so as to enable the members perched on the brink of one or the other of these gaps to be brought across the bridge into the desired 'One Zambia, One Nation?' Increasingly one notices, for example, that social occasions such as weddings, funerals, etc., are sources of non-communication between one generation and the next, and one wonders what needs to be done.

The problems sketched here represent only a fraction of the many problems that ought to be taken into account in one's consideration of the most relevant response to the multilingual situation such as obtains in Zambia. However, before going on to consider what needs to be done, in order to bring about meaningful national integration, it might be useful to take a brief look at how Zambia appears to have responded to its multilingual problems so far.

The response so far.
Up to this point only brief references have been made to the distinction that ought to be made between two related types of integration, political and sociocultural. This distinction is important if one is to understand the response that has been given, up to now, to the question of national integration in Zambia.

To recapitulate, political integration has to do with the efficient and effective administration of a state (i.e., 'operational efficiency', to use Fishman's term), whereas sociocultural integration is conceptually associated with the process of shaping and reshaping existing disparate ethnic (or cultural) units into nationhood (i.e., 'cultural authenticity' again to use Fishman's terminology). One thinks of sociocultural integration then as the process whereby existing sociocultural attributes of the people involved are remoulded and strengthened, or new ones evolved and given a meaningful national outlook. The result is that supra-ethnic (or national) modes of behaviour, loyalties, and institutions are evolved.

In terms of a nation's response to the two requirements, namely political and sociocultural integration, we often find that decisions that emphasize the political operational efficiency of the state are expedient, stopgap and temporary in nature. On the other hand, decisions that put emphasis on sociocultural integration (or cultural identity) appear to require long-term and well thought out plans. This reflects the (long-term) nature of the problem itself.

If we take Fishman's three models of the types of decision likely to be made in a multilingual society, Zambia would appear to fit 'Type A' or 'Type B'.[1] As posited by Fishman: -

Type A decisions are those which come about as a result of consensus (at least in 'leading circles') that there is neither an over-arching socio-cultural past (i.e. no pervasive feeling of unity of history, customs, values, or missions traceable into the reasonably distant past) nor usable political past (i.e., no pervasive tradition of independence, self-government, hallowed boundaries) that can currently serve integrative functions at the nationwide level. It is felt by elites in decision-making capacities that there is as yet no indigenous Great Tradition (no widely accepted and visibly implemented belief-and-behaviour

28

*system of indigenous validated greatness) that all or most of
the inhabitants can immediately draw upon to make them one
people and their country one nation.* (Fishman, 1971: 30-31).
Fishman advances further that the lack of perceived sociocultural
integration at the nationwide level, and the lack of felt political-
operational integration at the nationwide level, lead to the early and
relatively unconflicted arrival at Type A decisions, i.e., the selection of
a language of wider communication as the national or official language,
which is almost always a Western language and the one in use during
the colonial period (p. 32). As he sees it, 'the selection of a (usually
Western) language of wider communication and the continuation of a
Western trained *elite* [is] justified by the basic need to obtain as much
tangible aid, as much trained personnel, and as much influence abroad
as possible in order to meet the immediate operational demands of
nationhood' (p. 33). It is clear from this that it is operational efficiency
that is considered to be paramount and therefore vocally articulated
and emphasised in Type A decisions.

However, in the context of our discussion, it might be more useful
at this point to apply a simple test which would enable us to compare
the underlying philosophy that seems to prevail in countries, such as
Zambia, making Type A decisions, with that which appears to guide
countries, such as Tanzania, making Type B decisions. It must be
borne in mind, though, that comparisons presented here represent
a very simplified, and possibly a somewhat distorted, picture of the
true situation. It must further be remembered that whereas in Zambia
there is no indigenous (or indigenised) *lingua franca* that could
have served as a neutral rallying point in the selection of a national
language, Tanzania had a very convenient choice in the presence of an
indigenised *lingua franca* - viz, Swahili.

Decisions represented by Zambia	Decisions represented by Tanzania
1. Ultimate aim: National. Integration	1. Ultimate aim: National Integration.
2. Operational efficiency paramount.	2. Cultural authenticity (identity) paramount.

29

3. Cultural authenticity subordinate	3. Operational efficiency subordinate.
4. A Language of Wider Communication, viz English, to prevail and hopefully to become eventually the national language,	4. An indigenous (indigenised) language – Swahili chosen as the national language, but English to continue for a while for certain major official purposes, e.g. higher education.
5. As an expedient measure, a few indigenous languages to be used for limited (official) operational purposes	5. By design, all other indigenous languages to play no official role for the operations of state.
6. By default or by benign neglect indigenous languages (though never officially articulated) fall into disuse.	6. By deliberate policy, all other indigenous languages to give way to the national language in most spheres of communication.

There are several areas where decisions represented by Zambia, and those represented by Tanzania, coincide in their emphasis on operational efficiency and in their preference for an eventual monolingual situation. For example, Tanzania, in its choice of Swahili as *the lingua franca* that would enable the country to communicate most widely, appears to have felt that the decision would ensure operational efficiency, whilst at the same time it would facilitate the evolution of a greater national sociocultural consciousness.

At the same time, like Zambia, it would appear that Tanzania felt that the existence of many diverse languages hindered effective national integration, and for that reason, one may conclude, it deliberately excluded the active use of indigenous languages from government controlled national operations. As one Tanzanian paper put it:-

A common indigenous language in the modern nation states is a powerful factor for unity. Cutting across tribal and ethnic lines, it promotes a feeling of a single community. Additionally, it makes possible the expression and development of social ideas, economic targets and cultural identity easily perceived by citizens. It is, in a

30

word, a powerful factor for mobilisation of people and resources for nationhood (The Nationalist, 1968).

The decision to continue with English as the official language in Zambia was, and continues to be, clearly motivated primarily by considerations of operational efficiency. Mr Valentine Musakanya, then the Minister of State responsible for the Commission of Technical Education and Vocational Training, was undoubtedly expressing more than a personal opinion when he observed:

In the pursuit of [national] strength and progress the trappings of syllabuses searching for national identity must take second place and those in search of universal identity and the applicable knowledge ensuring national technical capability must take the first place (Musakanya, 1970: 37).

On the other hand, the areas where considerable divergence of approach is evident between Zambia and Tanzania, are those to do with the emphasis placed on the language of wider communication (English in Zambia and, to a decreasing degree in Tanzania, and now to an ever increasing extent Swahili in Tanzania), and the role or roles assigned to (other) indigenous languages concerning the official functions of the State. For sociocultural reasons, for example, Tanzania appears to have foregone, in the long-term at least, certain advantages which are believed to accrue to the use of an international *lingua franca*, such as English. Temporarily at least, Zambia on the contrary regards those advantages (coupled with the absence of an indigenous *lingua franca* such as Swahili in Tanzania) as the prime factor for selecting and maintaining an international *lingua franca* as its main official language.

Fishman describes in detail an important characteristic of nations, such as Zambia, which tend towards Type A decisions. Because this characteristic is central to our present argument I shall quote it here in full:

Bilingualism is viewed as having no nationwide function by the elites tending towards Type A decisions. It is not a characteristic of their ideal 'citizen of the future'. Bilingualism, widespread though it is, is viewed as having only a transitional role and even that primarily for two populations: the very young and the very old. The former manifest what we might call 'reading readiness bilingualism'. They have not yet fully encountered the institutions of nationhood: the school, the Government, the military, the higher culture. After this encounter occurs it is expected that their bilingualism will decrease. The old, on the other hand, are viewed as having already passed beyond major interaction with the interactions of nationhood. In both instances, what is expected is bilingualism en route to monolingualism. The young are expected to give up their local tongues in exchange for the nationwide (and increasingly national) language, which is also usually a worldwide Language of Wider Communication (Fishman, 1971: 35).

Moreover, in these countries the 'image of the national future tends to be monocultural rather than bicultural' (p. 37). While one may not agree with Fishman in every detail of his argument, his central proposition that what is expected is bilingualism *en route* to monolingualism, and that the tendency is towards culturalism rather than multiculturalism, merits further and serious consideration. Are monolingualism and multiculturalism - both aspects of homogeneity - the only honourable road to the future? For Zambia, and countries like it, this is the unanswered question.

NOTES

1. For a detailed discussion of the typology of decisions which are possible and which are therefore likely to be taken in multilingual developing countries, see Joshua A. Fishman's 'National Languages and Languages of Wider Communication in the Developing Nations' in W.H. Whiteley (ed.) *Language Use and Social Change*, London: Oxford University Press, 1971. Type C is not discussed here because it is not germane to the issue.

2. My subordinating operational efficiency to cultural identity in Tanzania might raise strong objections from those who feel that Tanzania is as concerned about the effectiveness of its state's operations as Zambia is. This is indeed undeniable. However, I am using 'subordinate' here to imply the greater willingness on the

part of Tanzania, as compared to Zambia, to emphasise, at least for the time being, the sociocultural identity of its people even at the expense of operational efficiency.

3. Despite the reported moves by Tanzania in 1984 to return to renewed greater use of English in education, especially as a medium of instruction, the basic position of Swahili as a national language remained largely unassailed. The long-term aim still, discernibly, remained that of developing Swahili as the premier language of government business and a vital instrument of facilitating national communication and therefore assisting the process of national integration and social cohesion.

CHAPTER 4
THE PATH TO NATIONAL INTEGRATION*

In seeking an honourable road to the future, or more specifically in the search for an acceptable compromise between our past on the one hand and our present and future on the other, there are important questions of which those of us in multilingual countries need to remind ourselves. Primarily, what we are concerned with when discussing the problem of language and national integration is the question of our entity as a nation, i.e., what is popularly referred to as 'our national identity.' What is it that makes us Zambians as distinct, say, from Tanzanians, Nigerians, Ugandans, Americans, or whatever nationality it may be? Is it the mode of our speech, the timbre of our voices, or the bulk of our build? In this connection, it is pertinent to ask: what distinguishes the Americans from the British? Is it language – British English versus American English? And if so, why are Australians, New Zealanders, and Canadians separate nations when they are bound together by a common language? In our case, does the mere fact that we are provided with the opportunity to communicate among ourselves throughout the country through the medium of a common official language, English, make us Zambians? Or is there much more to being Zambian than this?

Let us assume for the moment that we had no common geographical boundaries or common political or administrative systems. The question to ask is: what else would make us Zambians? What are the characteristic bonds that bind us together as a people? And, if minus geographical and broad political considerations, we admit that we don't have anything else in common, i.e. we do not consider ourselves to be already one people, what are the processes that should transmute us into a 'nation'? And if one can talk of 'language engineering', 'cultural engineering', or 'social engineering', is it similarly possible to speak of 'nation engineering'? What strategies can one adopt to achieve the desired, i.e. unattained, nationhood? And when, finally, this 'nationhood' *is* attained, what material objects, social and cultural

* First published in 1990 in *The Factor of Language in Zambia*.

facets of life, philosophies, literatures, etc., shall one consider to be 'national'?

It seems to me that one needs to consider whether, for example, Kafue is a *national* river (because it belongs to Zambia), or whether it is a *regional* river (because it is found only in one region of Zambia). Similarly, is the Lusaka-Mongu road a *regional* road (because it traverses only a particular portion of the country), or is it a *national* road (because, apart from being constructed from public, national funds, it belongs to the nation and stands to benefit all Zambians)?

Also, one has to decide whether a national literature is that written by *all* Zambians, or whether it is simply that written by one writer who happens to be *Zambian,* but which stands to benefit all Zambians. There is also the question of whether a book written in *one* Zambian language is *tribal* and not *national* literature. Which raises a further question: should one consider as *national* literature only that literature which is written in English – the so-called 'common' language? And how should one regard a song sung in Kaonde by Kaonde speakers (not necessarily Kaonde 'tribesmen'): as a *tribal* song (because it is sung in a 'tribal' language) or as a *national* song (because it belongs to the nation and stands to benefit all Zambians)? And what constitutes a 'national philosophy': that propounded by *all* Zambians, or that believed in by *all* Zambians, or that propounded *in* Zambia and which has the potentiality to benefit all Zambians?

This seemingly tedious catalogue of questions is important and is intended to alert us to the complexities and ramifications inherent in any discussion of national integration. It clearly points to the dilemma: whether on one's way to national integration, and in one's definition of 'national', one should make allowances for diversity and exploit it to one's advantage, or whether one should look upon diversity as a dangerous, sentimental luxury, and therefore always opt for homogeneity.

For the purposes of the present argument, I believe the important operative phrase is 'benefit all Zambians'. Are Zambian languages regional (or 'tribal') languages because they are spoken only by a portion of the Zambian population, or are they 'national' languages in the sense that not only are they now properties of Zambia (like the people who speak them), but, far more important, they can be used by, and therefore stand to benefit all Zambians? The response we give to this question would largely determine our attitude to the proposals that follow, proposals intended to suggest a practical framework within which a meaningful programme of national integration, for a multilingual Zambia, could take place.

One finds it difficult not to agree with the view expressed by Whiteley who admonishes that 'language planners must not shrink from exploiting the linguistic and cultural diversity of their countries; it should be regarded as a source of wealth rather than a threat to unity' (Whiteley, 1969: 109). I believe that in our diversity, despite its problems, lies our national strength, greatness and richness, but only if we recognise diversity as a national asset and consciously encourage its positive exploitation. I believe also that so far, in our preoccupation with the negative manifestations of ethnic particularism, referred to in Africa as 'tribalism', we have tended to give greater weight to the negative aspects of our diversity at the expense of its more positive attributes. Nobody would deny the dangers that are inherent in diversity, particularly in societies where negative attitudes are assiduously cultivated against it and consciously built into the political and cultural philosophies that are evolved to guide those societies. Zambia is an example of a society where a religion, so to speak, has quite consciously been evolved and elaborated against diversity.

If we accept that diversity is in many respects a national asset and not altogether a national liability, then it only remains to show how we could harness and utilize it in Zambia to our best advantage, with particular reference to Zambian languages. The best way to go about this would be to take our existing institutions and consider the manner in which each of them could employ Zambian languages, in complement to English, to promote national integration.

Literature in Zambian Languages

On January, Wednesday 3, 1973, an article appeared in the *Zambia Daily Mail* in which Esther Annan, a Ghanaian, expressed her feelings thus:

*Africans [have] lost ties with one another and unfortunately
this dangerous condition still exists.*

*There is no direct link between some of our countries today
because of sheer indifference and unreasonable suspicion and
even the little they know about themselves is handed down to
them by racist foreigners. My experience revealed this morbid
situation to me. In Britain, I met a Zambian who invited me to
meet other Zambians at Manchester University. The gentlemen
were very nice but they were shocked about the ignorant
questions I asked about their country. I did not know there was
a university in Zambia. That day I suffered the bitterest pangs of
disillusionment. On the other hand, I knew practically everything
about Britain and could tell them where to go and where not to
go. Africans must be selfseeking! Instead of trotting to Europe
for enlightenment, we could enhance our culture and brush up
one another's knowledge of Africa by frequent interchange of
ideas and visits.*

If the need for an interchange of ideas seems urgent at the continental
level, it is no less urgent, and in fact it is embarrassingly so, at the
national level. Consider, for example, a school anywhere in Zambia
(except where the *Ambo* live, or where other Zambians live near the
Ambo) at which a Social Studies teacher asks a class to tell him who the
Ambo are, where they are found, and their way of life. One of two things
is likely to happen: either there will be complete silence (an eloquent
testimony to the ignorance on the part of the children) or the teacher will
be inundated with wild guesses (an equally eloquent testimony to the
ignorance of the Zambian regarding his or her fellow-Zambians). Or if
the teacher has an intelligent child in the class, he might even be asked
back an intelligent question: 'Who are the *Ambo*, teacher?'

This illustrates that within their own borders Zambians have little
knowledge of their neighbours, where they live, how they live, and their
relevant place in the Zambian society as a whole. It is to be doubted
whether it is healthy for African countries to concentrate on educating
their peoples only about how people outside the national boundaries
live, simply because some of us feel, perhaps, that in our promotion
of knowledge, increased emphasis on the whereabouts and various

modes of life of our different peoples might amount to little else than a course in 'tribal differences'. The provision of informed insights into the music, languages, folklore, customs, beliefs, etc., of other Zambians would not be an unfortunate emphasis on the 'differences' in our nation as it is sometimes suggested. On the contrary it would be a sign of national maturity, a recognition of our diversity and an appreciation that in diversity might in fact lie our future greatness. An exposure of the Zambian to how other Zambians live is advantageous, in that it might reveal to him or her the rich treasures that are hidden in the variegated social and cultural systems of his or her own country, and might make him or her appreciate that diversity also has its good points.

It is mainly for this reason that I have often argued that it would be in our national interest if, in future, official encouragement could be given to increased exchange of ideas through literature in Zambian languages, to complement similar efforts currently being made, but so far almost entirely, through the medium of English. One notes with some satisfaction that the Social Studies being prepared by the Curriculum Development Centre (CDC) of the Ministry of Education are paving the way to, and are providing the formula for, the kind of information that should be disseminated much more widely about ourselves than is the case at the moment. Literature in Zambian languages provides an avenue so far grossly overlooked for effective national integration. In future, it would no doubt pay dividends if efforts were made to translate worthy works in one Zambian language into other Zambian languages. In this way, even those without an adequate knowledge of English, and who are presumably therefore literate only in their own languages, would have the opportunity to read and learn about other Zambians through their own language. The present widespread (unwritten) convention of Zambians writing in their own languages only about topics of interest primarily to their particular ethnic community is detrimental to our national well-being. For one thing, it gives Zambian languages a 'tribal' outlook. For another, it perpetuates a narrow outlook. Through English one is able to read and therefore to learn about other Africans, Asians, and Europeans, and this is in fact one way in which the language has, over the years, been able to shed its 'tribal' character and to assume an 'international' one. In the same way, I would advocate the expression, for example, of Lozi history, Lozi customs, Lozi folklore, etc., in Bemba, and *vice versa*. This is one of the more meaningful ways in which we can build relevant and permanent bridges of understanding between our respective peoples.

The School System
In our multilingual countries, there is a tendency to assume that existing multilingualism (i.e., the presence of many languages in the country) would eventually give way to monolingualism (i.e., the population eventually speaking only one language). Zambians tend to fall into the same trap. It would be interesting to see then what the actual trend is in the country: whether the signs are pointing to multilingualism *en route* to monolingualism, or whether the trend is in the direction of increasing multilingualism (i.e., individuals speaking two or several languages). As Graham Mytton, a former Broadcasting Research Fellow at the University of Zambia, has been able to show, we have tentative evidence suggesting that in Zambia the trend is very definitely towards ever increasing multilingualism. Using some of Mytton's data, the picture appears as follows:[1]

Table 1: Multilingualism and Age

Age	Average Number of Languages Spoken by the Individual
15-24	2.2
25-34	2.3
35-44	2.2
Over 45	1.9

Table 2: Multilingualism and Level of Education

Education	Average number of languages spoken by the individual
No education	1.6
Grades 1-4	2.4
Grades 5-7	2.6
Form I-II	3.4
Form III and above	3.2

This evidence suggests that while the acquisition of the ability to speak several languages does not appear to be directly related to age, increased multilingualism is definitely related in important ways to the level of education. It is evident, for example, that a person with no education is likely to speak fewer languages than a person with, say, a Grade 4 education. Similarly, a person with a Grade 5 education is likely to speak fewer languages than a counterpart with a Form II education. This would suggest that rather than the trend pointing to eventual monolingualism, available evidence in fact points in the opposite direction. And, though relevant figures are not shown here, multilingualism due to geographical mobility (the social phenomenon of people moving from one part of the country to another) appears to be even more significant. Geographical mobility, as we know, is at present most pronounced among school children and also among adults employed in the public service, so that it and the variable of level of education are closely related.

Meaningful language policies should, where possible, reflect realistic trends. That is, they should reflect phenomena and developments that at least bear some resemblance to reality. In the case of Zambia, it seems clear that it would be more meaningful and perhaps of greater value to society if adopted language plans and policies could aim to intervene in a positive way in the direction that trends in social and cultural development indicate. For example, here we have a clear instance, in our multilingual situation, of increasing multilingualism. Greater opportunities in education, widespread geographical mobility, urbanisation and inter-marriages, all seem to point to increasing multilingualism. And if that is so, as seems evident from what we have shown, would it not be a more realistic policy if official efforts were deliberately directed from their current emphasis (if clandestinely) on promoting monolingualism to that of promoting multilingualism?

Here, as a proposal, one merely needs to reiterate the suggestion that the Zambian government ought to consider substituting its current programme of teaching Zambian languages primarily to mother tongue speakers for that of teaching these languages to speakers of other languages. Such a programme would aim at ensuring that mother tongue speakers of Nyanja, for instance, are as the result of a deliberate policy required to learn Lozi, Kaonde, Lunda, Luvale, Bemba or Tonga in addition to English and, optionally, their mother tongue.

There are obvious advantages to derive from such a policy. Primary among these is the fact that it would generate greater opportunities for interethnic and interregional communication in the country. In other words, the officially approved Zambian languages would gradually cease to be seen as properties of particular tribes and would become truly national *linguae francae*. Secondly, they would enable Zambians to communicate with a variety of their compatriots: the old, the uneducated, and 'non-fellow-tribesmen'.

And in any case, there seems to be something disturbingly odd about the administrative practice in Zambia of transferring public servants from one region to another in a conscious effort to promote national integration, while on the other hand the same Zambia insists on adopting a deliberate policy of teaching Zambian languages along regional lines coincident, more or less, with boundaries popularly regarded as 'tribal' boundaries. We thus find that, as a government policy Nyanja is taught in the Eastern province while Tonga is assigned to the Southern province. No doubt there are justifiable, practical and educational considerations which prompted these policies. But in our planning for the future, it should be possible for a Chewa to learn Tonga in his or her own secondary school in the Eastern province, that is of course providing there is a competent speaker of Tonga *(not* necessarily a Tonga) to teach him or her. Presumably this would not be an insurmountable problem, especially in the coming years, since in any case Zambia has a parallel programme of posting Zambian nationals anywhere in the country.

The Public Service
In a vociferous contribution to "Varsity Corner" (*Times of Zambia,* 1971), I argued that:

> On the matter of language alone, I must hand it to the colonial government and the missionary. Both of them exercised more perspicacity than we have. The colonial official was, for example, quick to see that, along with the policy of indirect rule,

the native could only be reached and 'manipulated' by making judicious use of his language. The District Commissioner and others like him were promoted and/or paid more if they mastered one or two native tongues. Using apparently the same strategy, the missionary quickly endeared himself to the natives – certainly much more than many of our local officers are able to do today – by immersing himself in their language and also by learning their customs.

There are numerous examples of practices from Zambia's recent past that one could justifiably condemn outright as 'colonial'. But there are also some *colonial* practices which arouse one's admiration. I count among them the former colonial practice of encouraging public servants to learn indigenous languages. While there may have been something regrettable – and therefore, perhaps, 'colonial' – in the underlying philosophy that the white official had to talk down to the native in the latter's tongue, there was at the same time something of practical value, and therefore commendable in requiring civil servants to communicate with the local population in the language they could understand. Even today, very often the public official can communicate with the average villager most effectively only through the villager's own language: development programmes can be explained to him most effectively if his language is used. In any case, again as Mytton's studies have shown, it is not the English language but the Zambian languages which are at present the more effective and the more widely used media of communication in the country.

Therefore, while it may be impracticable in Zambia's present circumstances to increase a public servant's salary, or to promote him or her for learning and using a Zambian language other than his mother tongue, as was the case in the colonial administration, there would be considerable merit in a programme in which overt official encouragement could be given to public servants who made a conscious effort to learn the language or languages of the area in which they were working. Such a programme would recognise that, as a means of wider communication, English has at this stage its limitations and has to be complemented by Zambian languages.

Moreover, in terms of national integration, it needs to be appreciated that the trouble with English as a possible integrating tool is in fact its neutrality. The use of English does not seem to touch the same kind of responsive chord in the interlocutors as when their own Zambian languages are used. Intuitively, and even experientially, we know that a Zambian responds much more warmly and with greater appreciation (or at least with less suspicion) if he is communicated to in his own language than if English - or for that matter a language foreign to him - is used. In this sense, increased use of Zambian languages among the population is more likely to bring about more meaningful national integration than an emphasis on English.

Broadcasting
In so far as operational efficiency is concerned the role of broadcasting is quite easily stated: it is to disseminate official information as widely and as accurately as possible to the population. Zambia is in the grip of an urgent need to develop (however development is defined), and broadcasting is seen as one of the more important catalysts for fulfilling this need. As far as national integration is concerned, however, the role of, let alone the rationale behind, broadcasting is not easily discernible. Indeed in many instances the actual practices are clearly contrary to the spirit of the national motto: 'One Zambia, One Nation.' For example, in his Research Report No. 5, p. 20, Mytton reports that:

> *Very often listeners will complain that the music of their own particular area is not played enough on the radio. A lot of the demands for separate languages to be introduced on the radio stems from this demand. One Chokwe listener said: 'Why can't we have Chokwe tribe on the radio so that we can hear our own music?*

The problem here, Mytton points out, arises from the tendency of language sections at the Zambia Broadcasting Services (ZBS) to operate like tribal groups and not to cater sufficiently for the other languages.[2]

This observation is of great significance to our discussion of the problem of national integration, revealing as it does a practice, or a tendency, among broadcasters who appear to assume that their function is to broadcast to a particular group and not to all the groups in the nation. Their philosophy about language would appear to be similar to that of the population at large, namely that languages are vehicles of communication only among ethnic communities (or 'tribes') immediately associated with those languages. Hence, one is led to conclude, their tendency to direct almost all the broadcast programmes to a particular section of the nation so that in effect programmes in the Bemba language, for example, become programmes for the 'Bemba tribe', Kaonde programmes for the 'Kaonde tribe', Lozi programmes for the 'Lozi tribe', etc.

Such an orientation is clearly out of touch with reality. For one thing, none of the seven Zambian languages at present broadcast on Radio Zambia is spoken only by the immediate members of the nuclear family called 'tribe'. On the contrary, the true situation is that each of these languages is spoken (or at least understood) by first of all, the members of the language groups related to the language and, secondly, by those who have learned the language as a second language. When these two types of speakers are compared, it may be found that the latter in fact outnumber those who speak the broadcast language as a mother tongue.

What we have then is a situation where the broadcast languages have ceased to be 'tribal' properties and have to a considerable extent become vehicles of wider communication, certainly well beyond the 'tribal' boundaries. For another, the existing language policy in Zambia as it relates to broadcasting was in any case never intended to benefit only particular sections of the population. In intention, the present policy of the Zambian Government of having only seven Zambian languages broadcast on Radio Zambia does not mean or imply that programmes in these languages are intended only, or specifically, for those whose languages have been chosen: the Chewa, Tonga, Bemba, Lunda, Lozi, Kaonde or Luvale. On the contrary, what is intended is that *ANYBODY,* whatever his or her mother tongue background, who speaks or understands any of the seven languages is welcome to listen to that language. The intention then is to make the seven languages as much as possible 'national' properties, or national *linguae francae.*

There is, therefore, clearly a need to depart from practices which have tended to stress the notion that broadcasting in Zambian languages is another form of 'tribalism' – this time with official blessing. There is a need in future to stress instead the role that broadcasting can play in bringing about greater national integration in the country.

One way of achieving this would be to minimise or stop completely the recurrence of complaints such as that made by the Chokwe listener. If broadcasting in the seven officially approved Zambian languages is intended for anybody who speaks or understands the language being broadcast, and that such a listener might presumably be from any sociocultural background, then it is clearly imperative, if national integration is the goal, that in future most of the radio programmes should be as national in outlook as possible. Considerable effort is being made on the General Service of Radio Zambia (where English predominates) to prepare and present programmes that have at least some national appeal – the reason being, presumably, the popular belief that national integration can only be achieved by means of the English language 'a common, neutral language.'

Similarly, on the Home Service or Radio 2 (where only Zambian languages are used), there should be greater social and cultural contact on the radio between one language group and another. It is not just a question of a token concession to the 'Mambwe' to allow them to play 'their' music on the 'Bemba' programme, or the 'Ila' on the 'Tonga' programme, or the 'Tumbuka' on the 'Nyanja' programme; the question is much more fundamental than that. It is a recognition that no one language group *owns* a programme.

For this reason, I would propose what might be considered a radical departure from Zambia's existing broadcasting practices. My vision of broadcasting on Radio Zambia is to institute the presentation of, for instance, more Lunda, Lozi, Luvale, Ila, Nkoya, Leya, Inamwanga, Aushi, Bemba, Lala, Tumbuka, and other language groups' music on the Nyanja programmes, and the adoption of the same type of procedure for the other broadcast languages. Everybody should feel that the seven official broadcast languages are there for them, and not just for a favoured, select few. I see also great merit, for example, in a Luvale person who knows how to speak Lozi and who is knowledgeable about Luvale social life presenting a programme in Lozi, discussing *'Life among the Luvale'*. Such an exchange of programmes across languages and language groups is a very important factor in our conscious effort to generate greater understanding between our respective peoples.

This proposal would necessitate complete, or at least a greater degree of, integration of the staff in the Zambia National Broadcasting Corporation (ZNBC) than is the case at the moment. In fact, consideration might have to be given to the complete abrogation of 'language' sections such as the *Bemba Section*, and the *Lozi Section*, and in their place the creation of subject-based sections, e.g., *Music Section, News Section, Drama Section,* etc."[3] In this way, talent from a variety of language backgrounds could be pooled together to greater advantage, and in the process greater cultural cooperation encouraged among the different language groups. At the moment, the language sections in ZNBC tend to work either in isolation, or at cross purposes, or seemingly in the interest of particular language groups, i.e., not quite in the interest of national integration.

I believe that if we moved away from these tendencies we could, with much advantage and credit to ourselves, employ Zambian languages to achieve meaningful and permanent national integration. However, there are certain preconditions that must be fulfilled before this could be achieved. The first precondition that comes to mind is that the policy makers, the administrators, and the actual broadcasters ought to reconsider the proper function of broadcasting in a multilingual society. They ought to see it, for example, as being much more than just a simple operation of disseminating information and providing entertainment to the intended audience. Further, they should appreciate that Zambian languages, if properly utilized, could play an important and effective role in national integration, but that, if handled as at present, their overall effect could be altogether negative and counter-integrative as it might lead to the intensification of sectional orientations and attitudes.

Conclusion
The purpose of the preceding remarks has been to suggest that language in multilingual societies is either a divisive or an integrative factor, depending on what type of language policies are formulated and how those policies are handled. In Zambia, language policies

on the whole, as I have tried to show, have tended to be divisive rather than integrative. However, the national motto, 'One Zambia, One Nation', requires that the Zambian nation takes a fresh, serious look at the existing policies, particularly as regards their possible reformulation, so as to render language in Zambia a positive and not a negative variable in national integration.

NOTES

1. For a more detailed discussion of these sociolinguistic phenomena refer to Chapter I of Language in Zambia, especially pp. 35-45.

2. Mytton has discussed some aspects of language and broadcasting *vis-a-vis* national identity at greater length in a paper 'Language and the Mass Media in Zambia' in Language in Zambia, Sirarpi Ohannessian and Mubanga E. Kashoki (eds.), International African Institute, London. 1978. pp. 207-227.

3. This idea is not entirely original. In the main I owe it to Dr. Mytton who initially proposed it as part of his recommendations to the Ministry of Information, Broadcasting and Tourism.

CHAPTER 5
LANGUAGE, TRIBE AND THE CONCEPT OF 'ONE ZAMBIA, ONE NATION'*

For the purpose of this chapter, an appropriate way to break the ice is to respond immediately to the misconceptions and biases that have continued to becloud a proper understanding of the relationship between language, tribe and the concept of nationhood.

Africa as a land of tribal societies

The first of these misconceptions is the view one has regarding the type of African societies that existed before the advent of colonial rule. The prevalent view of precolonial Africa is that of the predominance of tribally based societies, each wrapped up in its own cocoon of tribal culture, interacting little, if at all, with other tribal societies, and as often as not operating in an uneasy, precarious state of endless tribal hostilities. Certainly, the colonial history that I remember informed me incessantly that, before the arrival of the white man, Africa knew no peace, enjoyed no cooperation between one society and another, but was instead ravaged by internecine wars, had no developed systems of communication, and engaged only in a primitive barter kind of trade. European intervention, the history of the day pontificated, had the immediate beneficial effect of putting an end to intertribal fighting, of introducing *Pax Britannica,* of promoting modern trade, and of teaching Africans new forms of government.

Alongside this general notion of a warring precolonial Africa is the related proposition that African communities prior to the coming of the white man lived in total, or almost total, isolation from each other. As Godfrey Wilson, an early observer of Zambian communities, put it: 'a tribe ... was not a community like a nation state; it was a loosely linked system of similar, tiny and relatively autonomous local communities. It was almost a world in itself, a homogenous world, and its contacts with neighbouring tribes were slight.' (Godfrey Wilson, 1941: 11).

*First published in 1973 in *The Bulletin of the Zambian language Group*

This view of Africa wishes us to believe that until the white man graced the *'Dark Continent'* with his exploring boot, there was no long-distance trade, no intertribal communication, no intermarriage, no military pacts, no cultural assimilation, no cooperation between one community and another, and above all no concept of nation or nation state. There was only intertribal strife and a life of perpetual fear. All these good things, long-distance trade, intertribal communication, peace, intertribal marriages, cooperation, and the concept of nation, the white man brought with him and bequeathed to the Africans. These are the positive spin-offs from the colonial experience. These are why the African should be grateful for having been colonised.

This belief has persisted up to the present day, and not surprisingly is being peddled, vocally, by the Africans themselves. For we are still being constantly told, (often by our own politicians and intellectuals), as we work within the notion of modern African nations, that it is only in modern times, particularly in the modern urban contexts of Africa, that one finds an explicit expression of political and social co-mingling of African peoples. Our rural areas are considered still too tribal and too homogeneous to constitute useful melting pots for the concept of nationhood. At the very core of this belief is a view of precolonial Africa without nations, peopled only by tribes. A view of precolonial Africa as being composed of autonomous, isolated, warring tribes is clearly intended to convey the message that the notion of 'nation' was not possible within these circumstances. It is an imported commodity. It was brought by European colonisers. They taught it to the Africans. It is another beneficial product of the colonial experience for which Africans should be thankful despite the difficulties they may be having in welding their various peoples into one people.

But we now know that this could not be so, and much historical evidence has been accumulated to give the lie to the view that until the white man arrived, as African societies we did not trade, we did not communicate, we did not intermarry, we did not enter into military pacts, we did not form political alliances, we did not change citizenships. We have ample evidence to show that Africa had important trade routes; it had kingdoms; it had empires; it had political entities larger than the tribe; it had nations; it had social and political links between one community and another; people belonging to different ethnic communities married; people speaking different languages communicated across tribal or other social boundaries; tribes on occasion went to war and some combatants died, while others were taken as slaves to be eventually absorbed into the sociopolitical structure of their captors; conquests, political alliances and military pacts resulted in the formation of social structures larger than the tribe. These things formed the sociopolitical scene of Africa and were the realities of Africa as a continent at the time. Though a specific word to convey the modern sense of 'nation' may have been absent in African languages, the concept itself was not. In practice, many African nations existed without a term applicable to those entities being present terminologically.

In Zambia, polities such as those of the Lozi and the Bemba, to give only two examples, were very much akin to the contemporary notion of 'nation'. These polities included members drawn from various ethnic communities. These polities, in other words, incorporated, absorbed or assimilated members from various ethnic communities within the context of empire, or that of 'nation'. As part of the process of incorporation, we know, for example, that certain people who came in as slaves eventually became full citizens of the social organisation into which they were absorbed.

Close to Zambia, in other parts of Africa, we know of the Luba and Lunda empires which flourished during the 15th and 16th centuries in the Upper Congo basin in present day Democratic Republic of the Congo (DRC). Similarly, in Zimbabwe, a Rozwi/Karanga empire is known to have flourished at about the same time. These were not tribal social organisations. They were entities larger than the tribe. They involved social and political relationships of a non-tribal nature. They involved interethnic relations, like in present-day Zambia.

In addition to our knowledge of the existence of these polities, in the not-too-distant past, we have evidence to emphasise the point that societies which were socially or culturally homogeneous were the exception rather than the rule. In the past, as in the present, Africa has been a land of multilingualism, of interethnic interaction, of empires, of complex political structures, of nations. The notion of a culturally homogeneous tribe in Africa was given its present concrete expression by the cultural anthropologists of the 19th and 20th centuries, who, coming from Europe where such notions were prevalent at the time, came looking for such characteristics in the societies which they found in Africa. The anthropologist, with the aid of the colonial government, fossilized African communities into their present rigid tribal forms. It was only after this artificial fossilization that the tribe in Africa seemingly lost its dynamic capacity. Before colonial fossilization, the African tribe was always in a state of flux, always changing, always adding to, or subtracting from, its membership. The African tribe, as a social structure, was never a closed system. Individuals married into it or married out of it. On occasion, individuals from other ethnic communities sought political asylum, were granted refugee status and eventually became fully absorbed as members of the community. Sometimes, the head of a community, fearing for the safety of his people, would apply for membership in a military or political alliance dominated by another community which was perceived to provide immunity from external attacks. Thus, alliances akin to NATO and Warsaw pacts were not unknown at that time.

To bring the foregoing to a conclusion, the argument so far has emphasised the importance of recognising that the lessons the new nation of Zambia can learn are not those only to be derived from Europe. There is much from Africa's own past that Zambia can learn. Zambia can go back to its sociocultural past to ascertain how African forms of government functioned, the type of politics that existed, the legal systems that operated, how citizenship was acquired and exercised, how social and cultural integration was achieved and how communication was carried on within the context of empire, or political alliances, or trading partnerships. I believe that such an exercise would have much to teach us, would be closer to our way of life, and would permanently dispossess us of the self-damaging misconception that nothing of relevance to our modern way of life can come out of Africa. The object lesson to be underlined here is that nations have been a part of our cultural life, and not at all a European import, and we should seize on their characteristics to guide us in our present efforts to make Zambia a viable modern nation.

African tribes and African languages as closed systems

At this stage, it is pertinent to return to a misconception which continues to generate misunderstandings of consequential proportions insofar as the triple concepts of language, tribe and nation are concerned. The dominant theme in this misconception is that Africa is inundated by tribal languages. An extension of this misconception is that as long as Africa has tribes and tribal languages the goal of 'One Zambia, One Nation' will be difficult to achieve. In other words, as was observed earlier, tribes and tribal languages are perceived to be serious stumbling blocks to nationhood.

How does this view arise? It arises primarily because of a general belief which perceives tribes and African languages as closed, impermeable systems. For example, in an imaginative attempt at drawing a distinction between languages of wider and narrower communication, Ali Mazrui (1975: 70) invents two interesting terms, 'communalist' and 'ecumenical', to apply to these two types of languages. In his own words:

Communalist languages are race-bound or tribe-bound, and serve to define as communities those who speak them as mother tongues. Ecumenical languages are extracommunalist, they transcend these boundaries of racial or ethnic definition.

He goes further to make his point more explicit: 'Communalist languages are those, like Luganda and Luo which can be used to define a race or a tribe'.

This view is shared by Chinua Achebe who argues in a similar vein, but whose point of reference is African literature. Achebe, as cited by Mazrui (1965: 217), defines 'national' literature as that which is written in what he calls the 'national' language, and 'ethnic' literature as that written in African languages.

What Mazrui and Achebe have done, of course, albeit in somewhat different ways, is to hold the English language flag aloft as the only language that can transcend tribal boundaries and to condemn African languages as being, exclusively, the property of tribes.

Mazrui, however, does make the important concession that 'communalist languages could be highly absorptive in the sense of allowing even newcomers to the language to be categorised racially or tribally as native, provided they have, in fact, succeeded in being linguistically assimilated' (p. 70). But the main point here still is that, despite their absorptive capacity, Mazrui continues to see them as essentially communalist or tribal languages. This runs counter to my own stand, which has been to take the opposite, and perhaps extreme, view that there are no tribal languages in Africa, or elsewhere. Tribal languages, by definition, can only be those which are acquired and spoken by members of a particular social group.

It is to be greatly doubted whether there is a language anywhere in the world which is spoken exclusively by members of a particular social group. In particular, there is no evidence of an African language which is spoken exclusively by the so-called 'tribesmen'. The only languages that I am aware of are those, however small, which are learned and spoken by members and non-members alike of the social group associated with that language. In the nature of things, languages – all languages – are acquired and spoken by two sets of people: native speakers and non-native (or second-language) speakers. In both these instances, the individual concerned need not be a member of the community immediately associated with the language in question.

Since we are here engaged in a debate of practical implications, let us put this proposition in a specific social context. If we take in Zambia the Eastern province and Lusaka as two of the geographical areas where Nyanja is predominantly spoken, we cannot say that in these areas the only native, first language, or mother tongue speakers of the language, are those belonging to the Chewa tribe or even to the Nsenga tribe, two of the social groups in Zambia more readily associated with Nyanja. Native speakers of Nyanja can be drawn, and are in fact drawn, from any ethnic group. Even some Asians have been known to speak African languages natively, not excepting Nyanja. Does this make them tribesmen?

Another good example in Zambia is the Copperbelt province. In the urban environs of the Copperbelt the predominant *lingua franca* is Bemba. Bemba is so predominant on the Copperbelt that children born and reared there tend to grow up speaking it as their first language or mother tongue. Irrespective of the ethnic origins of the parents, these children grow up to claim this language as their mother tongue.

Similarly, Lozi in the Western province, Tonga in the Southern province, and Lunda, Luvale and Kaonde in the North-western province cannot be said to be acquired as mother tongues only by tribesmen. These languages, like any other language in the world, are open for acquisition by any individual whatsoever, irrespective of ethnic or racial origin. In essence, no tribe or social group of people owns a language. A language is a national resource to which one has access either by virtue of acquiring it purely by accident as a native speaker, or by learning it as a second language. In either case, it is a neutral resource, the property of no one in particular. Strictly speaking, languages do not belong to particular sets of people.

Translated into more obvious terms, Mandarin as a language is up for grabs as a first language to any individual who is born and brought up in an environment where Mandarin is spoken. It is by means of this process that millions of people unconnected with the English tribe have come to speak English as a mother tongue and to claim it as their own, but without going to the extent of claiming membership in the English tribe. Mazrui's proposition that to speak Luganda natively is a sufficient condition for entry or acceptance into the Ganda tribe must therefore be rejected, for in the same way that native speakers of English do not become English tribesmen, to the same extent a non-Muganda native speaker of Luganda does not become a Muganda tribesman.

The counter proposition just stated is to call attention to the need to draw an important distinction between language and tribe. In Zambia, because of the confusion that prevails around these two terms, one finds many Zambian nationals pointing fingers of favouritism at each other for matters that should not be blamed on language or tribe. For example, presently one of the most politically sensitive debates in Zambia concerns the amount of broadcast airtime allocated to the eight official languages of the country, English, Bemba, Kaonde, Lozi, Lunda, Luvale, Nyanja and Tonga. In the general belief that language and tribe are one and the same thing, charges and counter-charges daily fly around the country to the effect that certain Zambian tribes have more airtime on the radio than other tribes. The fact of the matter of course, is that, if the distinction is maintained between a language and a tribe, then no single tribe in Zambia has any airtime on the radio. Only languages are broadcast on the national radio, not tribes. When English is being broadcast, nobody proceeds to proclaim that English tribesmen are squatting in Zambia's radio air space. However, as soon as any of the Zambian languages finds an hour on the nation's radio there is a rush to prominent political anthills to denounce tribal favouritism. The reason for this, of course, is that while few associate English with the English tribe, most people find it is very difficult in their mind's eye to separate language from tribe when the language in question is an African language. They cannot get away from the conception of African languages as tribal languages.

To put it more directly, the essential argument is that Cinyanja on Radio Zambia is not for the Chewa or the Nsenga; it is for the individual who speaks or understands that language. Similarly, Icibemba was not put there on Radio Zambia for the exclusive pleasure of Bemba tribesmen; Bemba programmes are for anybody who speaks or understands Bemba. The same philosophy operates for the other five Zambian languages officially included on Radio Zambia.

In this instance, then, the concept of 'One Zambia, One Nation' is undermined – seriously undermined – not because languages and tribes, perhaps too many languages and tribes, exist, but mainly because of a general ignorance of the prevailing facts. The languages and the tribes are essentially neutral in the matter.

It is our languages and our tribes that disunite us
From an imprecise understanding of the relationships between language and tribe, we move to another, and perhaps the most critical, area of misconception. This time we come face-to-face with the complex issue pertaining to the various negative 'isms' – favoritism, nepotism, regionalism, provincialism, tribalism, etc. – which daily affect social and political relationships in Zambia. One is here particularly concerned with the general assumption that these 'isms' are really the result of the existence of tribes and languages. The common view is that if only we were not plagued by too many languages and too many tribes the Zambian house would be in order and there would be less domestic squabbling amongst ourselves. Remove them and Zambia

is well on the way to restful sleep, contented stomachs and buoyant spirits.

Unfortunately, this optimistic thinking rests on very doubtful premises. I have often stated it, as a personal credo, that the point of departure for a more realistic appreciation of what is really at the heart of Zambia's present social and other differences is the scarcity of resources. At the centre of Zambia's current conflicts is the severe limitation of resources, resulting in a corresponding absence of equal opportunities, and the consequent manipulation and exploitation of whatever differences are manifest among her nationals as a useful tool for getting what they want.

The question needs to be asked: how is it that it is primarily those citizens who are more immediately affected by a competitive socioeconomic modern environment, who are preeminent in exploiting existing differences? How is it, as it has often been observed, that it is the national political leaders who appear to be preoccupied with fanning the fires of sectionalism? Why is it that the general elections are very much in danger of degenerating into an occasion for reminding the electorate as to who is, and who is not, their homeboy?

This is because those doing the reminding recognise all too well that the number of Cabinet posts is limited; it is because we cannot all become managers of parastatal organisations; it is because formal employment opportunities are not infinite; in short, it is because the national cake can only go to a lucky few. We are snarling and barking at each other, like hungry dogs, because we have to scramble for the little that there is to share. If we could all become prime ministers, managing directors, vice-chancellors or district governors, it would not matter to us in the least if we had one or a thousand languages. If we had abundant opportunities – enough resource for which to compete – we would not find it necessary to dig into each other's ethnic affiliations. There would be no point and no need.

What is a tribe or a language if you are comfortably housed, the recipient of a fat monthly salary, have all your children in school without having to shout at the headmaster, enjoy nutritional meals every day, and have everything that money can buy? That is to say, if opportunities were limitless, if we could somehow equalise them, i.e., if the national cake could fill everyone's stomach, your neighbour could not care less whether your name was Mbongombo or Lubangalala. On the contrary, precisely because your neighbour does not have a house; because your child has secured a place in Grade One and his has not; because he envies you your ministerial position; because you are the owner of a butchery and he cannot even buy a blanket your neighbour wants to know how your name is spelt, who your parents are, what language your mother speaks to you at home, and the manner in which you obtained the butchery. Your neighbour wants to know why you are fortunate and he is so disadvantaged. He has to find an explanation.

Thus, the absence of equal opportunities is basically our problem, not our tribes, nor our languages. Because of the current stiff competition among ourselves, today even provinces, which were created for administering the country, are suspect. Slowly we are moving from a position of "what is his tribe" to that of "which province is he from?"

This clearly suggests that when resources are limited, and opportunities are unequal as a result, any difference whatsoever will be readily pounced on for explaining why we have an adequate portion from the national cake while our neighbour does not.

This is an important lesson in itself. So long as inequalities exist in society, to that extent will any available difference be exploited to benefit the competitor. If it is not religious differences, then it will be class differences, or differences based on education, or on colour. As long as for most of us our livelihood continues to depend on the announcement of ministerial posts or managing directorships, the dirtier the general elections will become and the more loudly we shall ask where the successful candidates come from. As long as the national cake remains inadequate, the keener we shall be interested in the ethnic or provincial origins of our competitors. The key to the effective removal of our current social and political conflicts lies in our ability to eliminate inequalities and to equalise opportunities, not in eliminating tribes and languages. Our tribes and languages are scapegoats and no more. Our real enemy is our inability to equalise opportunities.

CHAPTER 6
VARIETY IS THE SPICE OF LIFE: THE PLACE OF MULTILINGUALISM IN THE CONCEPT OF 'ONE ZAMBIA, ONE NATION'*

Introduction

When tackling a topic as philosophically complex as that to be discussed in this chapter, it is perhaps helpful right at the start for one to lay the cards on the table so as not to leave, whether deliberately or inadvertently, one's persuasions, biases or attitudinal orientations in doubt. In my case, my philosophical leanings, and therefore attitudinal dispositions, incline me to embrace David Smock and Kwamena Bentsi-Enchill's contention (1975, 976: 5) that:

> The preservation of some loyalty to particularistic groups is not necessarily incompatible with national integration. Ethnic loyalty and national integration do not represent fixed irreconcilable points on a continuum, for national identity is not an all-or-nothing proposition.

I am equally attracted to their other persuasive philosophical proposition that the most appropriate response in many situations will probably be the promotion of inter-ethnic reconciliation and equilibrium 'rather than an effort to obliterate ethnic distinctions and forge complete national unification' (Smock and Bentsi-Enchill, 1975, 1976: 14).

This philosophical standpoint agrees with my own philosophical persuasions as when, for example, I pose the rhetorical question (Kashoki, 1990: 28):

> whether on one's way to national integration and in one's definition of 'national', one should make allowances for diversity and exploit it to one's advantage, or whether one should look upon diversity in our circumstances as a dangerous sentimental luxury, and therefore always opt for homogeneity.

It should always be borne in mind in this regard that nature and life itself (as essentials to the well-being – in fact to the very existence – of

---

* First published in 1977 in *Zango* 21, 11.

the human being) are a complex tapestry of variety or diversity and are characterised by mutually interactive or reinforcing harmonies and disharmonies, consonance and dissonance. This is to say that at the heart of nature – or life, if you will – are both order and apparent disorder, accord and discord, equilibrium and disequilibrium, uniformity and diversity, which all translate into one apt phrase: *'variety is the spice of life'*. Indeed in the nature of things both predator and prey represent a good example of the manner in which different natural forces act upon each other to result in the natural order of things as we know them.

Matter of Definition

What has just been stated brings us logically to matters of definition, for in matters of this kind, it is important and useful that one's moorings are established before expounding further on one's line of argument. So let us now confront the critical issue of definition in the form of a series of rhetorical questions. Basic of all, one may well ask, what is meant by 'nation'? And immediately related to this, what precisely is envisaged by the national motto 'One Zambia, One Nation'? Or, stated another way, what is intended to be achieved by processes leading to 'national integration' and 'national unity'? And, in any case, strictly in definitional terms, what exactly does one mean by 'national integration' and 'national unity'? What kind of product, whether social or political, is expected at the end of processes of national integration and national unity? This is to say, by 'national integration' or 'national unity' does one have in mind the presence or absence of diversity (i.e., the maintenance or removal of differences)? And if the latter is the case, what is to be dispensed with, how and why?

The manner in which these rhetorical questions are given helpful or relevant answers is critical to the consideration as to what should be the place of multilingualism in the concept of national integration or 'One Zambia, One Nation'. For depending on the definitional responses that are given, a comprehensive language policy that does not fully take into account the phenomenon of multilingualism is not possible, or at best is difficult to conceive. For instance, depending on the philosophical underpinnings informing the country's language policy, one may ask: what kind of citizen does Zambia, within the concept of 'One Zambia, One Nation', want to produce? A speaker of only one language (i.e., monolingual), or a speaker of two or more languages, (i.e., bilingual or multilingual)? Or at another level, what ought to be the role of all, and not just some, of the languages of Zambia in the process of national integration, and in that of promoting the nation's welfare generally?

It is, or it ought to be, clear from these rhetorical considerations that unless, in the first instance, there is a clear understanding in the nation of the terms or philosophical underpinnings involved, the path to the future can be considerably difficult to beat. Definitional clarity in this matter is consequently of supreme importance. This is particularly so as regards one's understanding or interpretation of 'One Zambia, One Nation'. Unfortunately, the national motto 'One Zambia, One Nation' as enshrined in bold relief on the national coat of arms gives rise to many assumptions and hence different interpretations. In the context of what is at issue here one has again to ask the quite pointed question: what exactly is meant or is supposed to be understood by 'One Zambia, One Nation'? And to underline a point touched on earlier, in one's quest for achieving the goal of one nation as underlain by the concept, how is one expected to handle the integrative process along the way, and what kind of national product is envisaged at the end of this process? That is, of course, if there is indeed an end to the process at all.

There are only two possible outcomes, as I see it, that can be conceptually supposed to derive from the process: it is either a nation altogether devoid of all differences or one characterised by a rich mosaic of social, political and other differences – in short, a nation of diversity and not uniformity. The question is: Zambia, which course do you wish to take in the context of 'One Zambia, One Nation' as your national motto?

A Brief Note on the Linguistic Setting in Zambia

Before proceeding further, it is perhaps useful at this point to provide a brief sketch of the linguistic setting in Zambia. This is in order to give a bird's-eye view of the language situation as it prevails, or as one observes it at the present moment, as well as to provide a backdrop to what follows later.

The first major point to underline is that in common with many countries in different parts of the world, both within and outside Africa, Zambia is a multilingual nation state in the dual commonly accepted senses of the term. In one sense, because of the fact that several languages or dialects are used for daily communication among the Zambian people, Zambia is a multilingual or plurilingual country. In the second sense, from the point of view of actual patterns of communication (i.e., what the Zambian people do with their national stock of languages), Zambian nationals in general terms are either bilinguals or multilinguals. Put slightly differently, confronted with a multiplicity of languages in their midst, and challenged to communicate with as wide a spectrum of their compatriots as differing situations and circumstances require, the response of the average Zambian is to acquire a command of not just one, but two or more languages as a coping mechanism. Thus, to reiterate, Zambians on average are not monolinguals (or competent manipulators of only one language) but bilinguals or multilinguals. In this sense, they have embraced diversity as their guiding philosophy in responding to a complex linguistic situation in their country. But exactly how many languages are spoken in the country?

The difficulty in responding to this seemingly straightforward question is that we do not, within the rigors of science, possess foolproof instruments for determining what is a language and what is not a language, or what is a *'dialect'* as against what is a *'language'*. However, what is easy to deal with is the removal of a fallacious myth very widely and tenaciously held in the country. Contrary to popular opinion, Zambia does not have seventy-three languages any more than it has seventy-three 'tribes'. This pervasive erroneous notion arises, as I have pointed out countless times before, from the prescription by the Zambian government of seventy-three tribes as the officially approved number of social groups designated as 'tribes'. The notion of tribe is then extended to the notion of language, the effect being that over a period of time almost everybody comes to accept, without question, that there are seventy-three languages spoken in the country, a number which corresponds exactly with the number of tribes officially approved by the government.

But what, then, is the language situation in the country? Bearing in mind what has already been stated, namely that we do not as yet possess an accurate scientific formula for drawing precise boundaries between a *'dialect'* and a *'language'*, it is fair to say that within the limits of our present knowledge, there are about eighty dialects (or varieties of language) indigenous to Zambia. These are the varieties of the total linguistic stock available for communication by the Zambian people and which can be reduced to anywhere between twenty to twenty-five distinct languages using such measures as vocabulary, correspondence, and mutual intelligibility as determinants of similarity or dissimilarity. But the more important point is that what we have here quite clearly, whether at the level of *'dialect'* or *'language'*, is an instance of linguistic diversity. This, as in other spheres of our national life, is characteristic of our Zambian society. We also find non-Zambian languages in use alongside Zambian languages as a means of communication in the country. English is notable in this respect. In the private lives of non-Zambian nationals, besides English, a fair number of languages such as Zulu, Ndebele, Hindi, Urdu, French and Italian are spoken at home and even at social gatherings. This adds to the linguistic complexity, or multiplicity of languages in the country, thereby strengthening the role of diversity as a dominant feature of the tapestry of Zambian society.

Historical Forces at Play

The historical origins of the Zambian people represent yet another feather in the cap of our nation's diversity. Available historic-linguistic and anthropological evidence points to the conclusion that the Twa of the Bangweulu, Kafue and Lukanga swamps are perhaps the earliest and therefore oldest inhabitants of Zambia. However, today in terms of language and culture, they have become assimilated into surrounding language groups. That is to say, they speak languages of their (more dominant) neighbours. The Twa were followed later by Bantu immigrants who originated mainly from the southern part of Zaire (the Democratic Republic of the Congo – DRC) and who subsequently settled in different parts of present-day Zambia, notably in the eastern, central, northern, western and north-western parts of the country. This migration process is thought to have been set in motion as early as the Iron Age (i.e., during the first centuries A.D.). This has given rise, in terms of present-day settlement patterns and linguistic groupings, to the presence of the Lamba in the Copperbelt province, the Lala and their off-shoot, the Swaka in the Central province, the Chewa, Nsenga, Kunda and Senga in the Eastern province, the Aushi, Luunda and N' gumbo in the Luapula province, the Bemba and Bisa in the Northern province, the Chokwe, Kaonde, Lunda and Luvale in the North-western province, and the Luyana group of peoples (e.g., Kwandi, Mbowe, Mwenyi, Kwandu and Mbukushu) in the Western province.

Social groups (more popularly referred to as 'tribes') not derived from the Upper Congo basin include the remnants of the Kololo, a Sotho offshoot from the south, the Mambwe-Lungu-Inamwanga cluster as well as the Nyika-Lambya-Wandya group in the Northern province whose origins can be traced to East Africa, (with the former having close linguistic affinities with the Fipa of Tanzania) and the Tumbuka group who are supposed also to have originated from the east.

The Tonga present a special and even a problematic case. Not having, as all other Bantu immigrants now resident in Zambia do, a strong oral historical tradition which can be relied upon in the difficult task of reconstructing an unwritten record, it is a moot point up to this day in historical, anthropological and linguistic circles regarding the exact origins of the Tonga. It is all, as a result, a matter of educated guesswork. Current theory, however, holds that like the Tumbuka, the Tonga are immigrants from the east, but concrete evidence has yet to be marshalled to support this tentative hypothesis.

The diverse origins of the Zambian people represent yet again the diverse character of the Zambian nation. In this regard as well, Zambia is rooted in a rich diverse historical background. This includes the historical fact that the Ngoni, a Zulu offshoot from South Africa, who today reside in the Eastern province and speak either Nsenga or Tumbuka as their vehicles of communication, crossed the Zambezi River in 1835 to form an additional strand in the complex mosaic of Zambian society. The more diverse the merrier, our history seems to say.

However, despite our assorted origins, we have at least one thing in common, namely our derivation from, and our belonging to, the *Bantu* stock of languages of the Niger-Congo family. In this one instance, except for the Khoisan hunter-gatherer nomads, the Hukwe and Kwengo on the fringes of the Western province on the border with Namibia, we are all children of one ancestor, an example of a common denominator in a vast sea of cultural and linguistic diversity. As a consequence of this, we are heirs to a common linguistic baggage, sharing a common pool of vowels, consonants, syllables, vocabulary and even the larger grammatical structures of our languages. In this particular instance, we are essentially 'One Zambia, One Nation' if common characteristics constitute the measure of the oneness of the nation.

A further characteristic of the Zambian nation, as we have seen, is the phenomenon of the languages that are acquired and used by the individual for (daily) communication. This is the multilingualism in the individual and not the multilingualism or plurality of languages used in the nation for communication. Once again here we are face-to-face with the phenomenon of diversity. The individual faced with a multiplicity of languages in the country says to herself or himself: 'to survive let me have a command of two or more languages as my coping strategy of communicating with my compatriots. Let me be a multilingual and not a monolingual. Let me practice the art of diversity'.

Political Pluralism, Multiculturalism and Multilingualism not Strange Bedfellows

This brings us to the next point. It is said that birds of a feather flock together. In this vein, I want to suggest, by way of drawing to a conclusion what has been said so far, that political pluralism, multiculturalism and multilingualism are birds of a feather and ought to be seen in that light when placed within the concept of 'One Zambia, One Nation'. That is to say, as in the case of plural politics, multiculturalism and plurilingualism ought to be approached from the same premises as those which accord central importance to diversity, or pluralism, as the cornerstone of democracy in the sense widely understood today.

Perhaps one way of stating the same thing in a different way is to make a brief reference to Robert Dahl's (1989: 18-19) characterisation of the conception and understanding of democracy by the Athenian Greek of the fifth century B.C. Robert Dahl reminds us that in the view of the Athenian Greek of those distant times, in contrast to our own circumstances, for democracy to prosper and endure the following factors, among others, ought to prevail:

(a) Citizens must be sufficiently harmonious in their interests so that they can share, and act upon, a strong sense of a general good that is not in marked contradiction to their personal aims or interests;

(b) They must be highly homogenous with respect to characteristics that would otherwise tend to produce political conflicts and sharp disagreements over the public good;

(c) 'The citizen body must be quite small;

(d) and finally, Citizens must be able to assemble and directly decide on the laws and decisions of policy.' As Dahl amplifies, 'so deeply held was this view that the Greeks found it difficult to conceive of representative government, much less to accept it as a legitimate alternative to direct democracy.

The image reflected in the Greek mirror of democracy is quite clearly altogether different from that which we see reflected in our own mirror of democracy. Ours, given our historical origins as a nation state, is a democracy founded upon, and hence rooted in, enormous geographical and population size and sociocultural complexity, or heterogeneity. As a consequence, the manner of managing our affairs – that is the form of democracy we desire – has to contend with not only the enormity of the space we occupy but also – in fact especially – with the diversity of peoples, customs, traditions, religions, and languages that are peculiarly characteristic of our modern nation states.

The very nature of our nation state has inevitably brought in its train the political and social problems that the Athenian Greek of the fifth century, B.C., sought to avoid. In our case, the very notion of democracy is rooted in the complex web of the difficulties and contradictions that are occasioned by the complex nature of our historical origins as a modern state. One particular difficulty the notion of democracy introduces in our circumstances is how best to rationalise the use of the multicultural fabric of our society, particularly the rich array of linguistic resources available to us as a multilingual nation. This, of course, is akin to the difficulty modern complex nation states face when deciding on the form of government that has the best chance of serving, efficaciously, the wide spectrum of interest groups found within the national boundaries, especially in order to obviate the danger of exacerbating conflicts which might lead to possible dismemberment, something we have seen happen recently in the former Soviet Union, Yugoslavia, and Czechoslovakia.

In the political arena, the answer in the liberal democratic tradition has been, characteristically, to opt for a multiparty and representative form of government. This formula allows for the various contending interest groups to rally around a limited number of political parties. These in turn serve as the springboards for forming the government –the elected oligarchy. From the same political parties come a few men and women who, by means of the political game of choosing representatives, proceed to become spokesmen or spokeswomen on behalf of the national population, the latter thereby entrusting the destiny of a nation to a select few.

This represents the manner in which democracy, as widely practiced today, has sought to confront the challenge of diversity. However, at times, as in our case during the Second Republic, in the search for an integrative model that places singular emphasis on 'oneness' in the belief that only this model is best placed to ensure a long-lasting, stable nationhood, we have witnessed approaches that preferred to resort to a single political party as the basis of democracy. This approach, in other words, saw the establishment of a one-party state as the solution to the political and social problems engendered by diversity.

In much the same way, in the linguistic arena, as different countries seek different solutions to their complex multilingual and multicultural situation, we have seen some countries opt for the selection and prescription of a single language as the only official and national vehicle of communication within the country. Tanzania, by resorting exclusively to the use of Kiswahili, provides a good, relevant instance of this. This approach quite clearly rests on the assumption that in the matter of national integration the selection and official use of a single language has the political magic of unifying a country made up of a multiplicity of sociocultural elements. Other approaches to the same problem, as for example, those of our own country, in contrast, opt for the use of two or more languages as official vehicles of conducting government, industrial and commercial business. This approach parallels that of forming only a few political parties as a way of reducing innumerable interest groups to a manageable number in the conduct of a country's political affairs. In this sense, both the formation of only a few political parties out of a multitude of interest groups, and the selection and official use of just a few languages out of a large stock of a nation's linguistic resources rests on the principle of governance by representation. This principle recognises that in complex nation states, not all the resources available to, or at the disposal of, the nation can be formally pressed in the service of that nation. Judicious, though by no means easy, choices have to be made. This is where the issue of an appropriate language policy arises. Democracy, in theory and practice, conjures up questions of fundamental human rights, of equality and fair play, of participation, and of regarding human beings, together with the fauna and flora within the boundaries of the country, as resources rather than as liabilities. Similarly, in a truly democratic state, the nation's languages (i.e., the entire stock of the nation's means of communication), ought to be regarded as valuable linguistic resources and as constituting fundamental human rights, as well as providing a wide array of media for citizens to utilize in the governing of their country. Here it is to be especially borne in mind that it is only through language, in particular the mother tongue, or the acquired languages that the individual is able to use functionally, that it is at all possible for freedom of expression, association, assembly, and movement to find meaningful practical fulfillment in a democracy. In this regard, it is hard to imagine citizens expressing themselves, and assembling, and associating with others, if they cannot functionally speak the language that is entailed in the acts of expressing oneself, assembling, and associating. Here then (in this context), it is reasonably easy to see language, in the dual perspective of a democratic fundamental human right, and as a valuable national resource.

Conclusion

The conclusion that has been drawn in the preceding section has salience, especially if the points that now follow are borne in mind, and serve as the launching pad for the sociopolitical action that is needed in the intricate task of shaping the philosophical direction of our country as regards the complex matter of language policy.

It is at once significant and instructive that in recent times, more particularly during the 1970s and thereafter, relatively well-established multi-ethnic democracies, such as those of Australia and the USA, which had earlier embraced an assimilationist or 'melting pot' model as their integrative panacea for their multi-ethnic and multilingual societies, have come to recognise the pivotal intrinsic value of multiculturalism and multilingualism in the sociopolitical management of plural nation states. This attests, at a more general level, to the growing recognition in the past few years in different parts of the world of the pertinence of multiculturalism and multilingualism as the very pillars of nationhood in the context of multi-ethnic nation states. As David and Audrey Smock have observed: 'national accommodation refers to a political strategy for communally fragmented societies in which the political system accommodates the communal groups at the same time that it attempts to promote a measure of common loyalty to the national community'. They then go on to make the cardinal point that:

In a political system in which communal groups have a sense of security and mutual tolerance, loyalty to the national community can be entirely consistent with the maintenance of the integrity of communal entities.

As a final point in this vein they would like us always to bear in mind that: 'national citizenship and committed membership should not be considered as irreconcilable alternatives' (1975: 14-15).

Apart from Australia and the USA, Canada too, has in recent years been in search of a more appropriate multi-ethnic, multicultural and multilingual character of the country beyond the mere prescription of English and French as the official languages of the country. To this end, it appointed in late July 1963, a Royal Commission on Bilingualism and Biculturalism whose multi-volume report, submitted between 1968 and 1970, approached the subject from such critical vantage points as language, culture, education, the world of work, voluntary associations, multicultural societies and federalism, among others. For me, the most persuasive proposition is that contained in Book IV, namely, '*The Cultural contribution of other Ethnic Groups (1969)*', which in part states that:

Integration, in the broad sense, does not imply the loss of an individual's identity and original characteristics or of his original language and culture. Man, is a thinking being; severing him from his roots could destroy an aspect of his personality and deprive society of some of the values he can bring to it. Integration is not synonymous with assimilation. Assimilation implies almost total absorption into another linguistic and cultural group. An assimilated individual gives up his cultural identity and may go as far as to change his name. (Royal Commission on Bilingualism and Biculturalism, 1969).

For myself, in line with this presentation's conclusion, are two equally fundamental cognate propositions, the first being that every human language as an individual's basic human right deserves to be protected and promoted, a measure very much in the interest of maintaining linguistic diversity in a vibrant, multilingual society. This is also to argue that, as in the case of other forms of diversity, the rich diversity of a country's languages should be seen as a source of national strength, rather than as a national problem calling for elimination measures. Linguistic diversity, as a reflection of the varied cultural diversity of a country, needs to be husbanded and nurtured, not nipped in the bud. How this is done, however, is the challenge which calls for an appropriate national response. There is no doubt that it is at the level of policy that diversity, in whatever form, becomes a critical variable in the attempt by plural nation states to bring about viable, national integration.

Closely allied to the principle of language as a fundamental human right is the understanding of language as a national resource. The perception of social phenomena in this manner would lead to the abandonment of the sociopolitical standpoint which has tended in the past to view the existence of a multiplicity of languages in multilingual nation states as necessarily a major obstacle to national integration. The opposite should be the case. As has already been argued, multilingualism should, rightly, be seen as a social reality and as constituting a manifestation – nay, an essential part – of life's diversity.

It is part of variety as the spice of life.

CHAPTER 7
LANGUAGE, COMMUNICATION, AND NATIONAL UNITY IN ZAMBIA INTO THE 21ST CENTURY*

Introduction
In the interest of simplicity and coherence of treatment, this chapter is divided into three parts: the first dealing with the prevailing language situation in Zambia; the second with observable patterns of communication in the country; and the third with questions of national unity, with particular reference to the manner in and the extent to which language phenomena impinge on the factor of national unity.

A Sketch of the Language Situation in Zambia
Available knowledge in the scientific world does not enable us to state with exactitude how many distinct languages form the means of communication in Zambia. This is because we do not as yet possess precise conceptual or methodological instruments of determining what is, and what is not, a language. But let us at once rid ourselves of a fallacy or, at any rate, a misconception.

The notion that there are seventy-three languages in Zambia simply because the government has officially, but without any scientific basis, decreed that there are seventy-three tribes assumed to make up the Zambian nation is utterly erroneous, a perpetuation of historical misinformation and socio-linguistic inexactitudes. Zambia does not have seventy-three tribes, any more than it has seventy-three languages. What exists in Zambia are putative tribes. As in the case of language, no precise formula has so far been devised by social scientists by means of which one can draw precise boundaries between one set of people and another set of people and designate them as distinct 'tribes'. In any case, even if indeed seventy-three tribes did exist in Zambia, it would not automatically follow that there were seventy-three languages in the country. As we shall see later, there is not always a one-to-one

* First published in 2007 in the *Journal of Humanities.*

correspondence between language and tribe. In other words, there is no such infallible equation as tribe = language or language = tribe.

In the Zambian linguistic context two factors, among others, render it difficult to arrive at what can be accepted by everybody as distinct languages. The first has already been stated, namely the lack of agreement on the definition of 'language'. Nobody has yet invented, or devised, a neat and precise trick for measuring and determining distinct languages.

The second factor has to do with the relationship between the so-called 'dialects'. In Zambia, what we have is a complex linguistic mosaic. Whether we choose to call what we speak a 'language' or a 'dialect', what is characteristic of, and notable in, our situation is the close relationship that exists among the indigenous stock of languages or dialects that are found in Zambia, with one or two exceptions. All the indigenous languages spoken in the country belong to the Bantu group of languages. In their relationship, they exhibit to varying extents close phonological, morphological, syntactical and lexical degrees of correspondence. That is to say, it is not always the case that a Zambian language sounds as unintelligible noises to the next person.

When all this is taken into account, it should be understandable why one has to be extremely cautious, and somewhat ambivalent, in stating how many distinct indigenous languages are found in Zambia. However, using our present crude instruments of measuring linguistic differences, we may, as a conservative estimate, put the number of what may be considered distinct languages at about twenty, and the number of their variants, or dialects, at approximately eighty. Only the future, when more precise means of measuring linguistic differences are devised, may give us a better opportunity to reformulate with greater precision our present knowledge as it pertains to matters of language.

Up to this point attention has been more narrowly focused on what are categorised as 'indigenous languages'. But Zambia is not an isolated country; it has become, especially in the years following her independence, part of an international community. In these circumstances, it is inevitable that languages from across her borders should also be spoken in the country, however minute the degree of actual use may be. We can, therefore, be sure that, particularly in the privacy of the home, but also in the playground, the golf course or even in business offices, such languages as German, Italian, French, Portuguese, Gujarati, Hindi, Urdu, Kiswahili, Shona, Ndebele, etc., form an auxiliary part of the total package of languages that facilitate communication in Zambia.

Note that, quite deliberately, English has up to this point been excluded from the list above. The reason is simple and obvious. English, as a non-Zambian language, occupies a special place in the affairs of Zambia as a nation. English in Zambia at present, because of prevailing linguistic policies, happens to be the dominant official language. It is the pre-eminent language of education, government, as well as commerce and industry. In more recent years, as a result of more widespread use, it has even made significant inroads into the informal social activities of the people. English on an ever increasing scale is being extended in its use to the ordinary lives of the people, not excepting the intimate areas of love letters and romantic whispers. Even the privacy of the home has not been immune to this encroachment of the language on the ordinary lives of the people. In many a home today, particularly in urban areas, one will find some, and sometimes only, English being used by members of the family.

But English is not the only official language of the country, as is often mistakenly supposed. Seven Zambian languages, Icibemba, Silozi, Kikaonde, Lunda, Luvale, Cinyanja and Chitonga, have also been prescribed as official languages. These languages are officially used on the national radio, in education, for the dissemination of official government information, and for the promotion of literacy in the country. The fact that they are a poor second to English in terms of the status, prestige and attention accorded to them does not in any way negate the fact that nevertheless they, too, are official languages.

We have thus, in effect, two sets of official languages: English, which is assigned a more strategic and prestigious functional role, and Zambian languages, which are relegated to a comparatively peripheral, functional role. However, even within the context of this dominant/ subordinate relationship, English and Zambian languages complement each other in facilitating national communication. At present and in the foreseeable future it seems one cannot do without the other.

Patterns of Communication in Zambia

Logically, the preceding brings us to the question of actual patterns of communication in Zambia. If, when discussing matters of language, what is really at the heart of the discussion is communication, then it is not sufficient merely to enumerate the number of languages spoken in a country. This tells us very little about the actual use of these languages in the country. Rather, what is more important to know is: who speaks which language, in what numbers, in what domains or circumstances, and for what purposes? Only the answers to these questions would give one a clear perspective on actual patterns of communication in the nation.

Unfortunately, linguistic research in Zambia to date has not given us adequate answers to the entire range of these questions. In consequence, what we know is sketchy and rudimentary.[2]

What do we know so far? Perhaps the most important piece of information in our possession at present is the evidence that, in terms of actual language use, Zambians on the average are not monolinguals, that is, they are not citizens, as individuals, who have a command of only one language, or who are capable of manipulating only one language in their day-to-day communication. The opposite in fact seems to be the case. Zambians as a general rule are multilinguals, that is, individual citizens who know and speak several languages.

According to available information arising from a Mass Media Audience Survey conducted by Dr. Graham Mytton, from 1971–1973, under the auspices of the Institute for African Studies of the University of Zambia[1], we learn that, taking Zambia as a whole, Zambians speak an average of 2.2 languages. The average is even higher for the urban context. Mytton demonstrated that Zambian adult urban residents spoke an average of 2.8 (or almost three) languages as against an average of 1.9 (or approximately two) languages for rural inhabitants. A study of individual provinces, in this connection, was also very instructive. It is now clear from the information at our disposal that Zambians resident in our rural provinces are no less multilingual than their urban counterparts.

This can only tell us one thing: that Zambian people have been pragmatic in responding to a complex multilingual situation. Instead of restricting themselves to a competence in only one language, they have found, from a practical point of view, that they can only survive, in terms of communication, if they mastered and manipulated several tongues. This can be stated somewhat negatively: Zambians have found that English is not the panacea for all their communication requirements. Their experience has shown them that, in some social contexts, English may be the language to use while in others it would be utterly inappropriate, and in that case one or another of the Zambian languages would be clearly preferable. This is a situation which requires the individual to be eclectic and dexterous in the choice and use of the available linguistic resources, including the fact that in one conversation between the same speakers it may be necessary to alternate between English and a Zambian language, or even to mix them, thereby resorting to what among language experts is known as code-switching and code-mixing.

What we now know from the recent studies of the Zambian linguistic scene should also enable us to dispel a widely held myth, both at home and abroad, in social, political and even academic circles. The myth relates to a general notion that advances the view as axiomatic that all African languages by their nature are 'tribal' languages. There are two variants of this notion that are relevant here and which require some emphasis because they will have a bearing on our subsequent discussion of the concept of national unity. First is the assumption that African languages, being 'tribal', are the cultural property of the tribe that bears the same name as the language that is associated with it. By this token, the Luvale language, for example, is assumed to belong to the Luvale people and to nobody else. A related variant of this notion appears to posit the view that mother-tongue or first-language speakers of a 'tribal' language can only, or exclusively, come from the community of people associated with that language. Thus, to use *Luvale* as an example once again, mother-tongue speakers of *Luvale,* according to this gospel, can only be members of the *Luvale* tribe. A particularly disturbing aspect of this association of a given language with a particular social group, in the context of Africa, is the tendency to believe that there are no second-, third- or fourth-language speakers of African languages. Or, to put it more directly, the notion seems to suggest that African languages are linguistic tools that serve only a particular, clearly demarcated, social group as a means of communication. In other words, they are not languages of wider communication, that is, languages that transcend tribal boundaries in terms of widespread intergroup communication.

But what is the actual position on this score? Contrary to the implicit assumptions inherent in the notions as just discussed, recent language studies in Zambia show that, as a general rule, Zambian languages are not in-group tools of communication, restricted in their use only to specific sets of people called tribes. In the majority of cases, they are truly *linguae francae*, or languages of wider communication. As such, they are used in daily life by both those who speak them as a mother tongue, as well as those who speak them as a second, third or fourth language.

More recently Graham Mytton's findings have been supported by the sociolinguistic data that are contained in Chapter 4 of the '2000 Census of Population and Housing', (CSO, 2000) entitled 'Language and Ethnicity'. It **is** evident from these data that multilingualism, –the sociolinguistic phenomenon that indicates that the average individual in Zambia speaks two or more languages – is on the increase rather than on the decrease.

Moreover, as regards extent of use, Zambian languages show characteristics of spilling over ethnic boundaries and are to be found spoken hundreds, if not thousands, of kilometres away from the territory with which they are geographically associated. Present evidence also shows that the mother-tongue speakers of these languages are not necessarily tribesmen or tribeswomen. The speaker of a language could be anybody who, by accident or force of circumstances, was born or grew up in an area in which the given language is spoken as a mother tongue. In this regard, African languages cannot be said to be a peculiar breed of languages with a law unique unto themselves. They obey the same linguistic laws as are applicable to all other languages throughout the world. That is, what is true of English is also true of Zambian languages – they too possess an inherent capacity to capture speakers beyond the tribal boundary.

The Factor of National Unity

Before going on to talk about what the future holds in store for Zambia in the next decade and beyond, it is useful to make some cursory remarks regarding the question of national unity insofar as it is linked to questions of language and communication. Language and national unity in our part of the world are notions that quite often are easily confused. The reason for this confusion lies in the fact that, in the belief system of many people, the general idea is naively entertained that without a single national language national unity is not possible. We see an expression of this in American history as well. Until very recently, when the concept of the 'melting pot' has come into serious question, as we shall see later, the United States of America has ,since its own independence, believed in the sanctity of a single language, English, as a symbol of national unity. The social forces at work have been such that many immigrants from non-English-speaking countries who seek assimilation and acceptability in America have been compelled to change even the spelling of their names, so as to give them an English appearance. It is only today that **Zbigniew Brzezinski** can retain the original spelling of his name, whereas in the past the **Andersens** changed theirs to **Anderson.**

In Africa, in particular in Zambia, the need for a single national language as a symbol of national unity is accentuated by a parallel belief whose basic proposition is that full nationhood can only be achieved if perceived sociocultural differences, of which language is a primary one, are removed. When this belief is coupled with the related notion that African languages by their nature are tribal languages, and therefore the property of particular tribes, the compulsion to eliminate linguistic differences as a means of forging national unity becomes at once readily understandable. This is because, so perceived, African languages, instead of being regarded as assets in the development process of the nation, are on the contrary seen as barriers to meaningful national unity and an impediment to effective national communication.

In the early stages of the development of any nation, and America during its own early development was no exception to the rule, questions of national unity are exceedingly sensitive matters, because one's preoccupation is almost exclusively concerned with ensuring that the disparate groups that make up the emerging nation state are woven into the national fabric. It is at this stage that the various 'isms' (favouritism, nepotism, regionalism, provincialism, tribalism or ethnic particularism and racialism) loom large and take on a very menacing face. In the face of this assumed looming danger, it is natural that people should look for scapegoats. In Africa, all too often, the scapegoats are the African language and the tribe. The African language and the tribe become scapegoats for the nation's apparent lack of national unity because they are imbued with inherent divisiveness. The general assumption is that the 'isms' that plague Africa would not be such an intractable problem if only the tribes and their languages did not exist, or were wiped off the face of the earth.

The few issues discussed thus far prompt us now to ask: What are the prospects for Zambia in the next decade and beyond? It is to this dimension of the discussion that it is now appropriate to turn.

Prospects for the next Decade and Beyond
Predictive ingenuity is not a virtue with which I am endowed in any great abundance, but despite this handicap, I shall dare attempt a few tentative predictions as to what the future holds for Zambia in the next decade and beyond. I shall adopt the same format as I have observed so far in this discussion, that is, I shall divide the rest of this chapter into language, communication, and national unity.

(a) Language
The most pertinent question to ask here is: What is likely to be the language situation in Zambia in the foreseeable future? Or stated in another way: What languages are likely to be spoken in Zambia in the years to come?

To answer this question adequately, it is useful to divide the languages likely to be spoken in the country into two categories, official and unofficial[3]. At the official level, we are confronted with what may be termed the ideal and the practical. Concerning the ideal, the African Union, of which Zambia is a key member state is clear and categorical regarding its official stand that African independent countries should consider moving gradually to a position where

African languages are adopted as official languages, so that in time they can replace the current European languages, such as French, English or Portuguese, which presently play this role. Zambia as a member of this body endorses this view in principle, at least as evidenced by pious resolutions. At the practical level, however, there is understandable vacillation. Why? The answer is simply that there are many social, political, economic, psychological and other forces at play. Some of these we have already discussed. For the purpose of this brief presentation it is pertinent to cite a few of the attitudinal factors that account for the current reluctance on the part of African governments to consider African languages as worthy candidates for replacing European languages as the principal official languages of the state.

At the heart of the problem is the sheer multiplicity of indigenous languages in most member states of the African Union in a situation where a government has to choose an official language, or official languages, from an array of eager and jealous competitors. It is not an easy task to arrive at the optimal choice, acceptable to all. In such circumstances, it is considered politically advisable to reach for a language that appears to be relatively neutral. More often than not, the language considered as being neutral is a non-indigenous language, the consequence being that the legacies of colonial history are thereby perpetuated. Assumed neutrality is reinforced by the association of African languages with perceived potential political divisiveness. It is feared, among politicians and policy makers alike, that to select one or other African language in preference to several others, as the country's official language, could lead to political instability. This fear takes us back to the point made earlier, namely, that since African languages are perceived as exclusive properties of certain social groups, those social groups whose languages are not selected would immediately feel aggrieved, because they would regard the exclusion of their own language as representing a socio-economic disadvantage to themselves. Added to this is the perception of African languages, if selected and utilized for official purposes, as promoting inequality, a characteristic which is not associated, quite mistakenly of course, with the European language currently in use as an official language.

Three other perceptions require brief mention as further obstacles to the promotion of African languages as the principal formal tools of communication of the state. There is, firstly, the argument that the selection of African languages as official languages will not promote international communication, but instead will make the world a more difficult place to live in. It is further argued that the African language is not sufficiently technically developed as to meet adequately the needs of a modern society. The final argument states that the economic cost of modernising African languages is too high to justify the investment. It is less costly, it is felt, to stick to the European language currently in use.

While all these arguments can be countered[4], it will suffice to state here that given these prevailing attitudes, it is extremely doubtful that Zambian languages will in the near future replace English as the pre-eminent official language of government, commerce and industry. It seems more probable that, as at present, they will continue to play an official, peripheral role. As to whether or not the present seven official Zambian languages will continue in that capacity beyond the next decade is a foretelling that is beyond the magical powers of my crystal ball. Political decisions are hard to predict, and deciding what is, and what is not, to be an official language is essentially a political issue requiring a political decision. And, as is well known, political decisions are not always based on expert opinion, but rather more on grounds that are immediately practically (or politically) expedient.

Communication
In effect, to talk about Zambian unofficial languages is to talk about communication. A pertinent question to pose in this regard is whether or not unofficial African languages in Zambia will eventually die. The simple answer, of course, is that while it is true that languages can eventually fall into disuse, and Latin is a good example in this regard, it is equally true that languages are not in the habit of dying without putting up a spirited fight. They have a resilience of their own.

Even in the United States where English is dominant, such languages as Polish, Hungarian, Italian and Yiddish still have pride of place in the private home. In the Zambian context, we have seen that the trend, in terms of actual language use, is not tending towards growing monolingualism. On the contrary, what is evident is widespread and growing communicative multilingualism. This would suggest that for a long time to come Zambian languages will remain active as a means of communication among the Zambian people. One's prediction, therefore, is that in the next decade, and beyond, multilingualism will be on the increase, making it possible for Zambian languages to remain a vital and critical factor in the communication process of the country. Inevitably, however, some languages will decline in use following Darwin's theory of survival of the fittest.

National Unity

The national mottos of the USA and of Zambia are almost identical. Whereas the USA, obscurely using a defunct language, states its guiding national motto as *E pluribus unum* (Out of many, One), Zambia with more economy and succinctness proclaims its motto in the phrase 'One Zambia, One Nation'. The basic assumptions are also similar. For hasn't America (i.e. the USA) always regarded the American nation a melting pot in which the various strands of ethnic and linguistic entities (Irish, English. Scottish, German, Italian, French, African, Jewish. Native American, etc.), drawn from a multiplicity of immigrant and indigenous tribes, are expected to give way, and reach a fusion into, some metaphysical entity called the 'American nation'? And hasn't Zambia, before and during her independence, similarly always aspired to reducing her various ethnic and linguistic entities into the cherished 'One Zambia, One Nation'? The ideals of the two countries have also been more or less the same. Both the USA and Zambia have tended to assume that unity and harmony are fundamental to the well-being of their polities, and while to a great extent the concept of interest groups is considered an essential ingredient of the American democratic process, neither Zambia nor the United States explicitly accepts conflict or the existence of differences as a desirable, let alone an inevitable, fact of life. Indeed, as a generality, all countries desire to see that their people live in harmony and peace, while enjoying security, both of their person and their families. Conflict everywhere

81

is perceived as an unmitigated evil, despite its being a central feature of human existential life.

Given these national ideals and aspirations, what kind of Zambian national is likely to emerge in the years to come? The degree of national unity to be achieved in this country, or in any other country for that matter, in the 21st century is not a thing that can easily be subjected, with any exactitude, to predictive speculation. The best that one can do in the circumstances, therefore, is to extrapolate from prevailing observable social and linguistic trends and project these into the future.

It might be useful in this regard to look at four factors as our basis for further discussion. The factors I want to examine are the mother-tongue factor, the ethnic-affiliation factor, the residence factor and the marriage factor. All these have a direct bearing on questions of national unity, since they will in the years to come have a profound influence on the processes of national integration and social change in general.

At present, the general assumption, as we have seen, as regards the concept of mother tongue, is to associate a given language exclusively with a certain social group, or the so-called tribe. On the basis of this general assumption it is perfectly acceptable to argue that, because a person is *Lozi* by tribe, for example, his or her mother tongue is necessarily *Silozi*. However, while this may have been the case in the past, it will become less and less tenable, as the years advance towards the twenty-first century, to predict the first language, or mother tongue, of a Zambian citizen simply on the basis of the sound of his or her name. Even today, tribe and language are not always synonymous or interchangeable. The distinction between tribe and language will become even more marked as the twentieth century draws to a close. As at present, but even more so in the future, it is not always the case that because a person is ethnically Kaonde, his or her first language is therefore necessarily Kikaonde. A Kaonde can grow up speaking a first language other than that associated with his or her Kaonde social group. For various reasons, such as residence coupled with geographical mobility, this trend is likely to be accelerated in the years to come.

Closely related to this general assumption is a parallel assumption
which at its core seeems to rest on the erroneous notion that a person
from, say, Kasama must by that token be a Bemba. What this means is
that it is assumed that you can pin an ethnic label on a person by simply
asking him or her where he or she comes from. Thus, according to this
deductive philosophy, birthplace and ethnic affiliation are assumed to
have a direct correlation.

Even at present it is doubtful whether this assumption accords
with the facts. I have several Bemba friends who were born and bred
in Tonga land and whose first language is Chitonga, but who, by no
stretch of the imagination can, because of this accident of birth, be
added to the Tonga social group. Their ethnic affiliation continues to
be Bemba because they were born of Bemba parents. In other words,
they are Tonga by language and Bemba by ethnic identity. We see
this fact of life reflected more clearly in the United States. There,
Americans delight in using hyphens (Irish-American, Lithuanian-
American, Polish-American, African-American etc.) despite the fact
that Ireland, Lithuania and Poland may be only faint memories and
the hyphenated-American may not even be able to utter a word in
the language his or her forefathers spoke, because his or her first and
functional language now is English.

At one time in our own country's history we were witnesses to stern
warnings that were being issued from political platforms, no doubt as
a result of acute national frustration, that 'criminals in future will be
sent back to their rural or home areas'! Apart from 'rural or home
areas' in this context sounding like some kind of eighteenth century
Australia, to which unwanted English convicts have to be exiled,
a serious difficulty arises as to the definition of 'home areas'. The
present apparent understanding of 'home', as being the place from
which one's parents or grandparents came before migrating to the
urban areas, is one that will give rise to difficulties as regards practical
application in the decades to come. At that time we shall not so easily
be able to say 'the convicted criminal is a *Phiri*, so let us pack him
off in the prison van to Chipata' on the assumption that all *Phiris* in
Zambia have the Eastern province as their original home. Lusaka, and
only Lusaka by the year 2000 and beyond, may have become *Phiri's*

only home. And it may well be that the *Phiri* we intend to ship off to Chipata may in fact be the product of a Senior *Phiri* who has married a *Chanda*, a Bemba from the Northern province. Our special problem then will be how to regard the *Junior Phiri*. Is he Ngoni or Bemba, or perhaps some indeterminate, intermediate, or hybrid sort of human being, something between the two parents who brought him into the world? And what of his 'home': is he from Chipata, or Kasama? If he is to be rusticated to a rural home as a convicted criminal, which home, Kasama or Chipata, will be ready to welcome his homecoming?

It is not only the convicted criminal who will have difficulties tracing his home in the years beyond the 1990s. The aspiring Member of Parliament, too, will be confronted with similar problems of residential identity. Already we are witnesses to a political phenomenon whereby individuals who have been resident in urban areas for many years, and who have only a tenuous connection with the rural home of their birth or their parents' birthplace, are able to rush 'home' at election time in the hope of winning a vote as a 'homeboy' or 'homegirl'. In the 21st century, I doubt that the rural electorate will be so gullible as to readily embrace an aspiring candidate who was born and bred in an urban area. At that time, it is most likely that the aspiring candidate will not only be regarded by rural folk as an opportunist, but more so as a stranger who would have a better chance at the polls if he or she remained with his or her own kind in town.

A complicating factor in this dynamic social process is marriage. The annual University of Zambia (UNZA) Graduation Ceremony may, in one sense, be described as a tedious and boring ordeal because of the many hours one has to sit, stoically listening to the calling out of names of those upon whom the highly coveted academic degree is about to be conferred. For the more attentive and discerning, however, it can at the same time be a very rewarding experience in terms of what one is able to learn about Zambian society and the process of social change. For a name such as 'Python Blackwell *Chanda Phiri*' has much to tell us about social change in Zambia. Not only does such a name convey the message that English names, even unusual first names, have become common in Zambia, but more importantly, those familiar with the Zambian social scene are left in no doubt that the combination of *Chanda* and *Phiri* is a pointer to the fact that the *Chandas*, commonly associated with Northern Province, and the *Phiris*, generally regarded as originating from Eastern Province, are crossing ethnic and provincial boundaries to join hands in marriage. Nor should it be assumed here that this is entirely a characteristic of our times. On the contrary, interethnic marriages have been a social phenomenon from the dim days of our forefathers and foremothers. What is perhaps new is that it is taking place on an ever increasing scale during our own lifetime.

What does this social phenomenon portend for Zambia? The answer is simple. Without government intervention, and without the fuss of formal official policies, the Zambian people are doing their own thing. They are, unaided by government prodding, creating their own 'One Zambia, One Nation'.

Conclusion

In a more general way, it is in this informal type of social change, whether as regards language, patterns of residence, marriage, music, dance, theatre, etc., that one sees perhaps the more significant factor than formal government policies, in the overall national development of the Zambian people. It is clear from what the Zambian people do, and not so much from what they are formally directed to do by their government, that the Zambian nation will long remain a plural society. In the sphere of language, unless current social and political orientations radically change, English has an assured place, for years to come, as the dominant official language of the state. However, alongside this dominance, Zambian languages will hold their own, since they will for long remain the more effective means of communication in the ordinary lives of the Zambian people. Zambia will thus remain a multilingual, or plurilingual, society. I predict, too, that the tribe as an identity label will long endure. It has endured in America and Great Britain. But the persistence of the ethnic label will in no way negate or undermine the 'nationness' of the Zambian nation. 'One Zambia, One Nation' should not imply a total removal of differences. It should imply only an imaginative and positive accommodation of differences in whatever form.

What I see then is a constantly changing social panorama as expressed in changing communication patterns, residence patterns and increasing instances of intermarriage. These three factors, among others, are certain to have a profound and lasting effect on the future sociocultural fabric of Zambia. In particular, they are likely to be the chief and dominant determinants of a future Zambia into the 21st century.

Notes

1. For full details of the account of this study, see Graham Mytton's *Listening, Looking and Learning* Lusaka: Institute for African Studies, University of Zambia, (1974).

2. Refer to Sinarpi Ohannessian and Mubanga E. Kashoki (eds,) *Language in Zambia.* London: International African Institute (1978).

3. For a fuller appreciation of the prevailing sociolinguistic situation in Zambia, refer to 'Rural and Urban Multilingualism in Zambia: Some trends' *International Journal of the Sociology of Language* No. 34 (1982: 137-166); also, reprinted in *The Factor of Language in Zambia* (as chapter II). The Kenneth Kaunda Foundation (1990). See also Graham Mytton's *Listening, Looking and Learning* (1973), Institute for African Studies, University of Zambia.

4. For example, Chapters 1,2,3,4, and 11 of, *The Factor of Language in Zambia* attempt to grapple with the complex, sociopolitical questions of 'nation', 'nationhood', 'national unity' and 'national integration', particularly from the perspective of the multiplicity of languages in multicultural and multilingual modern national states.

REFERENCES

Australia, Commonwealth of (1984). *A National Language Policy Report by the Senate Standing Committee on Education and the Arts.* Canberra: Australian Government Publishing Service.

Brelsford, W.V. (1965). *The Tribes of Zambia.* Lusaka: The Government Printer.

Canada, Government of: Report of the Royal Commission on Bilingualism and Biculturalism (1969). *Book IV: The Cultural Contribution of other Ethnic Groups.* Ottawa: Queen's Printers.

Center for Applied Linguistics (1960). *Second Language as a Factor in National Development in Asia, Africa and Latin America.* Washington, D.C: Language Information Series.

Dahl, R. A. (1989). *Democracy and its Critics.* New Haven and London: Yale University Press.

Das Gupta, I. (1968). 'Language diversity and national development' In J.A.Fishman et al. (eds.) *Language Problems of Developing Nations.* New York, London, Sydney and Toronto: John Wiley: 17-26.

Deutsch, K. W (1966). *Nationalism and Social Communication.* Cambridge: M.I.T.

Fishman, J. A. (1968). 'Language Problems and types of political and sociocultural integration: a conceptual summary'. In J. A. Fishman et al. (eds). *Language Problems of Developing Nations.* New York: Wiley.

Fishman, J. A. (1968). 'Nationality – Nationalism and Nation – Nationism.' In J. A. Fishman et al. (eds) *Language Problems of Developing Nations.* New York: Wiley.

Fishman, J.A. (1971). 'National languages and languages of wider communication.' In W.H. Whiteley (ed.) *Language Use and Social Change.* London: Oxford University Press.

Kashoki, M.E. (1990). *The Factor of Language in Zambia.* Lusaka: Kenneth Kaunda Foundation.

Kashoki, M.E. (1995), 'Language, communication and national unity in Zambia in the next decade and beyond'. *Journal of the Zambian Languages Association* 1: 1-13.

Mazrui, A. (1975) *The Political Sociology of the English Language; an African Perspective.* : The Hague: Mouton.

Meebelo, H. (1971). *Reaction to Colonialism.* Manchester: Manchester University Press.

Molteno, R. (1974). 'Cleavage and Conflict in Zambian Politics: A study in Sectionalism.' In William Tordoff (ed.) *Politics in Zambia.* Manchester: Manchester University Press.

Musakanya, V.S. (1970). 'Technical and Further Education.' In *Report on First National Education Conference.* Lusaka: Government Printer.

Mwanakatwe, J.M. (1968). *The Growth of Education in Zambia since Independence.* Lusaka: Oxford University Press.

Mytton, G. (1973). 'Multilingualism in Zambia: An examination of data from a national mass media audience survey'. In the *Bulletin of the Zambia Language Group.* Vol. 1 No.2.

Ohannessian, S. and M. E. Kashoki (eds.) (1978), *Language in Zambia*: London: International African Institute.

Smock, A. C. and D. R. Smock (1975). *The Politics of Pluralism: A Comparative Study of Lebanon and Ghana.* New York/Oxford/ Amsterdam: Elsevier.

Smock, D. R. and Kwamena Betsi-Enchill (eds.) (1975/76). *The Search for National Integration in Africa.* New York: The Free Press.

Spencer, J. (1963). 'Language and Independence.' In John Spencer (ed.) *Language in Africa.* London: Cambridge University Press.

Whiteley, W.H. (1969). 'Language choice and language planning in East Africa.' In P.H. Gulliver (ed.) *Tradition and Transition in East Africa.* London: Routledge Kegan Paul

Wilson, G. (1941). *An Essay on the Economics of Detribalisation.* The Rhodes-Livingstone Papers No.5, Part 1. Lusaka: Rhodes-Livingstone Institute.

Printed in the United States
By Bookmasters